Secrets of Solo Racing

Expert Techniques for Autocross & Time Trials

D1009778

Henry A. Watts

Loki Publishing Company
849 Gary Avenue
Sunnyvale, California 94086
(408) 245-4040

ISBN Number: 0-9620573-1-2

Library of Congress Catalog Number: 89-092254

DISCLAIMER: The contents of this book are true to the best knowledge of the author. All recommendations are made without guarantee on the part of the author or the publisher. The author and the publisher disclaim any liability incurred in connection with the use of any data or recommendations in this book. In particular, no portion of this book should be taken to suggest or condone the violation of any traffic laws or the practice of any unsafe driving.

Other books by the author:

Car Beautiful, A Complete Guide to a Shiny, Well-Protected Car

Printed in U.S.A.

"It is not always possible to be the best, but it is always possible to improve your own performance."

——————— Jackie Stewart

"If you are under control you're going too slow."

——————— Parnelli Jones

"Most amateur drivers go too fast in slow corners and too slow in fast corners."

——————— Emerson Fittipaldi

"The driver who keeps the front tires the straightest will win."

——————— Anonymous

"When the green flag falls, the I.Q's go to single digits."

——————— Lee Chewey

"It is blessed to instruct others to do good, and no trouble either."

Mark Twain

Secrets of Solo Racing

Chapters

Table of Contents

Illustrations & Photos

Introduction

This is a handbook of solo racing. It introduces the sport to the beginner in terms that are understandable. It also should provide expert guidance to the advanced enthusiast. Writing such a book has been a daunting yet welcome challenge. The sports involved are enjoyable to the point of being seductive, and the joy experienced by people learning to drive better is always infectious. If you are reading this, you must be interested in competitive driving. Welcome to the club, and may you have a grand time.

If you are a beginner, this book is designed to ease you through the early stages of figuring out what is going on at the events, with your car and with your driving. It will also provide you with an introduction to skills and techniques that will make driving on the street both more fun and much more safe. If you already have some solo racing experience, you will find discussions of the driving and preparation techniques needed to become truly expert.

The book uses the terms autocross and time trials, but one of the major organizers of such events has different terminology. Autocross is known to SCCA (Sports Car Club of America) as Solo II. Similar events are sometimes called slaloms. Time trials are called Solo I by the SCCA.

This author strongly believes that people new to competitive driving should begin with autocross. The risks of damaging cars or people are extremely small in autocross, the costs can be modest, yet the opportunity to learn is essentially unlimited. Because of this, autocrossing is introduced first. After describing how events run, the book covers techniques of competitive driving, then how to prepare the car. If you have never been to an autocross, or if you are a student preparing to attend an autocross school, you may wish to skip the sections on advanced driving techniques and car modification the first time you read the book. Both of those sections will make much more sense once you have seen an event and had a chance to drive your car under track conditions.

The time trial enthusiast may wish to skip the chapters on how autocrosses are organized and how to work an autocross course. You will find useful information in all the driving and preparation chapters. Additionally, there are special chapters on driving at time trials and preparing the car for time trials. It is beyond the scope of this book to cover the extensive design and modification issues required of highly modified race cars, and there is a good body of literature to support people interested in such a level of preparation.

Fast, safe driving is not learned from a book. This book will help only if you practice the techniques, and spend time at events. Indeed, the fine points of some of the techniques may be difficult to understand for a driver with extremely limited competitive driving experience. Some of the techniques may take a competent driver years to perfect. Don't despair; remember that the key idea is to have fun and to improve over time.

No project as major as writing a book is completed in a vacuum. In this case there are many people who provided critical help. I am indebted to Dwight Mitchell, who provided extensive and valuable comments and Fred Puhn, who reviewed the entire manuscript and provided friendly and expert help with certain technical aspects of performance suspension and aerodynamics. Terry Zaccone, Vern Lyle, Dave Gershon, John Kelly, Pat Kelly, Lloyd DeMartini, Pattie DeMartini, Sara Webb, Richard Stuck, Jerry Hagn, David Wong, Tom Provasi, Ken Myers, John Byrne and Ray Scruggs all made important contributions. Without the expert publishing help (and faith in the project) of Tim Parker, Publishing Director at Motorbooks International, the book would certainly not exist. Rodney Rapson reviewed an early manuscript and provided very strong encouragement that was both welcome and, at the time, very needed. Joe Donahue, a dynamicist, provided technical guidance in certain critical areas. I am also most deeply indebted to Caren Chappell, Mike Low, Catherine Crisafulli and Laurie Webb, all of whom expertly proofread versions of the manuscript and provided extensive, patient and relevant guidance. The final decision on content (and grammar!) was mine in all cases. T.J. Dersch, the photographic genius behind MotoFoto, is responsible for all the photography. The graphics on the cover car were done by Alan McCaskey, general artisan extraordinaire. Enhancement for the cover photograph was provided by the retouching expertise of Lynne Turner. The graphics were all done by the author.

Henry G. Watts

A. *What is Solo Racing?*

On any given weekend morning, all around the United States, the careful observer can see, within the early morning traffic of people going to work, families getting an early start on a day or weekend trip, and a few laggard, hard-core party animals finally heading home, a subtle pattern. Part of this traffic is all going to the same place. The cars are sports cars, or sporty sedans. Their tires look a little wider than normal. Some of the cars look like they have been modified for performance. Some of them display stickers that say SCCA or Sunbeam Tigers Owners Club or such. A few cars, no longer suitable for driving on the street, are being towed on flat trailers behind vans, pickups or motorhomes. As the drivers see each other in traffic, they wave and smile, for this is no gathering of strangers. It is the gathering of the autocross clan for a day of fun and excitement.

1. What is an Autocross?: Autocross is the sport of trying to navigate your car through a defined course faster than your competition. It is a performance driving event. It is designed to accommodate cars ranging from sporty sedans through dedicated race cars. Autocrossing is a safe way to learn how to drive your car at the limits of its potential. It is also a sport that is accessible to many people. It does not require a large amount of money nor a willingness to take undue risks.

Autocrossing is <u>not</u> wheel-to-wheel racing, where all the competitors are on the track at once, passing each other as they are able and vying for position, sometimes bumping each other. Most of the differences between autocross and wheel-to-wheel racing are due to a desire to make autocrossing a safe and affordable way to race. Autocross is more of a test of a driver's ability to learn a course quickly, since each course is different and a driver typically gets just a very few tries at it. A typical run usually lasts less than two minutes.

> *Autocrossing is a safe way to learn how to drive your car at the limits of its potential*

In autocrossing the course is defined by soft barriers, such as traffic pylons, so cars that drift or spin off course are not damaged (in the way that a car might be damaged by drifting off a race course and smashing into a concrete wall or a tree).

Events are typically run at <u>relatively</u> low speeds (45-65 mph). On most courses cars will not be shifted beyond second gear. On the other hand, it is quite exciting. There are many interesting things a performance-oriented car will do in second gear at 65 mph or so.

Depending on how the event is being run, either there will be only one car on the course at a time, or the cars on the course will be well separated. There is essentially no chance that two cars will run into each other. On a closed (complete lap) course there will be two cars on the course at once, but they will be on different portions of the course

> *There are many interesting things your car will do in second gear*

and one car will be just finishing its run while the other is just beginning. On a start-here-finish-there course, there may be as many as three cars on the course at once, but they will be separated by a safe distance.

There are many reasons people autocross. Drivers able to handle their cars at the limits of performance are <u>much</u> safer street drivers when confronted with surprises. Because of this, autocrossers gain confidence in their driving. The social aspect is also important. It is generally a friendly competition, a social and educational gathering of friendly enthusiasts. The people tend to be active, practical and intelligent. Mostly, though, people autocross because they find it fun.

2. <u>The Autocross Day</u>: The day begins at an available large paved surface, normally a parking lot or a county airport. It begins early, as people from the sponsoring organization arrive to set up the course by placing pylons, marking a box around the pylons and, in some cases, laying down a chalk line to define both the right and left boundaries of the course. Grid areas where the cars will await

> *It is a friendly competition, a social and educational gathering of a clan of enthusiasts*

their chance to run may also be defined. Timing equipment must be set up and tested and a public address system is often used. A special area for safety-inspecting the cars may also be defined. The materials needed for registration will be set up on a table.

Registration happens first. During this time the course is usually available for the drivers to walk around; this is the best way to get familiar with the course before you actually run it.

At approximately the scheduled time, cars begin to run the course. This will continue more or less steadily throughout the day. If there is a lunch break, it will usually also be an opportunity for late arrivals to walk the course.

At the end of the day scores are tallied, the pylons picked up, the equipment put away and the autocross is over, except for the bench racing. Some groups have a tradition of gathering over pizza and beer (or other refreshments) after the event to discuss the happenings of the day, the great runs, the unlucky pylons and the success hoped for at the next event. This activity is called bench racing.

At essentially all autocrosses, the drivers are also responsible for doing the various jobs necessary to run the event. Since the same people cannot drive and work at the same time, various schemes have been devised to divide the driving time and the work time.

3. Time Trials: Time trials are solo racing at real road-racing tracks. They are run similarly to autocrosses, in that each driver competes against the clock rather than wheel-to-wheel against other drivers. Normally, there are practice sessions before the timed runs, where cars and drivers practice in groups. Since the speeds are higher than autocross, and the consequences of going off course much more severe, more safety equipment and driver certification is required.

4. Competition Classes: In all solo racing, drivers compete against other drivers in cars of similar performance potential. In each class, the driver with the fastest run in the class wins that class at the event. A class will have cars that are similar and which have been modified to about the same degree.

5. Levels of Competition: There are many levels of competition in solo racing. The most informal are often the autocross clubs associated with businesses or schools. Many marque-oriented (brand-name of car) clubs put on regular or occasional autocrosses, and some sponsor a time trial series each year. Racing clubs, such as SCCA (Sports Car Club of America), have both regional events and events that are part of a national series. The racing clubs and some marque clubs have once-a-year national events. SCCA also has a national Pro-Solo series, designed for professional autocrossers. CMC (Council of Motorsport Clubs) sponsors a national series similar to Pro-Solo. At the national level of the racing club events are professional racers who invest substantial time and money in the sport. But at the grassroots one can find the drivers who are having a grand time simply competing in local events. These drivers get a lot of enjoyment at relatively low cost.

B. How to Drive at an Autocross

"I was down to my last run of the day. I was behind by 3 tenths of a second, but only because I had hit a cone. All I had to do was drive the same, but not hit the cone. I could even slow down a bit, if needed, to be sure that I didn't hit the cone. I was sure I could do it. So I did a very smooth run, didn't hit the cone, and was <u>one and a half seconds slower than before</u>. Don't <u>ever</u> underestimate the difference between pushing really hard and pushing kinda hard!"

―――― Story from Terry Zaccone

1. Before the Event: Before the event, you must have prepared your car and yourself (see chapters G through J). You also need to know where the event is being held and what time your group runs. Plan to be at the track early enough that you have time to unpack, walk the course, and get ready with time to spare. Having to rush will impede your ability to concentrate properly.

2. Registration: When you first arrive, you must register. You will pay a small fee, sign an insurance release form (which holds the club and landowner blameless for essentially anything that happens) and sign up to work. You will probably get some literature about other events being sponsored by the club that is putting on this event. You may get a little badge (participation plaque) to put on your dash, and you may get a map of the course.

You will be given a registration card with your car number for the day. The registration form usually will have a technical inspection form on the back. Fill out the front of the card and tuck it under your windshield wiper or lay it on the dash just inside the left front window. The card will be completed when your car has been inspected, and then will be collected before the cars in your group make their first run.

If you have not run with this club before, now is a good time to pick up a rulebook. This will clarify specific procedures and help you determine what class your car belongs in with this club. Sometimes the books are free; in other cases you will have to buy them.

> *Pick up a rulebook*

3. Final preparation: Driving slowly, find a place to park, get the car unloaded, and do your final preparations. There are lots of people around, often including little children. Do not use even the remote sections of the pits for showing off or testing the acceleration or handling of your car. Once parked, take all loose objects out of the car.

This is a good time to check your tire pressures to determine whether you want to add some air to the tires. You should also check everything else about the car to be sure that it is as ready for fun as you are. If your windshield wiper controls are on the steering stalk, you may also wish to remove the windshield wipers, or pull the fuse for the wipers. In the heat of driving many a driver has accidentally turned on the windshield wipers. Once they are on you either have to let them run (they are distracting) or you have to take your mind off the course for a second to get them turned off. To minimize distraction, you may also wish to turn the side mirrors close to the car so you are not tempted to look back to see whether you actually hit that pylon.

4. Technical Inspection (Tech): Tech consists of a safety inspection of your car. The person responsible for the condition of your car is you. After you have some experience autocrossing, you should KNOW that your car will pass tech because you have already checked everything. The people at tech are really only a backup/enforcement system.

Sometimes cars are teched on grid, other times there is a special tech area. If there is a special tech area, take your car there and get it inspected. It is good to do this early, so you have time to resolve any problems that may arise. Tech personnel will be looking to see that you filled out the registration

> **The person responsible for the condition of your car is YOU**

card completely, that your tires are in reasonable condition, that your battery is secure, that your helmet has the required sticker (is not out of date), that you have enough brake fluid, that you have adequate seatbelts, that the car is not leaking fluids, that the front wheel bearings are sufficiently tight and other things of this nature. Note that tech inspection is not for classifying your car. You are responsible for classifying the car and marking the class on the registration form.

When your car passes the complete inspection, the form is signed off and put back under the wiper or on the dashboard. Your car number is written on a side window or in the upper passenger corner of your windshield with white liquid shoe polish. The number becomes a name for your car, it's identity while running. It allows you and the car to be identified and discussed by the announcer, course people and other officials.

If more than one driver is driving the car, the numbers of all the drivers will be written on the car. Be sure to remember which number is yours, as you will need to tell the person who is relaying this information to the timing people. Otherwise, some other driver in your car may get credit for that great run you are going to make. Some clubs prefer to have you tape numbers to the car doors on both sides of the car. In such cases you must display only one number at a time, so be sure you have your own number on the car when you run. In some clubs you can arrange to have permanent numbers. You can then paint them on the car (if you want to attract a lot of attention while you are driving around on the street), or make some nice numbers of magnetic material that can be applied and removed whenever you like.

5. Coursewalk: After the car is teched, walk the course. This is a critical step, for it is the first time that you can begin to assemble your plan of attack on the course. While you are learning, walk the course with an experienced driver. This is an excellent way to learn the specific course as well as learning what the experts look for. Examine the

> *Walk the course with an experienced driver*

surface so you will know where there are rough spots, bumps, potholes, oil spots, water puddles, and the like. Analyze each part of the course to plan where you want the car to be and what you want to be doing with it. Know where your turn-in points are and what apexes you are going to use (more about these topics in the next few chapters). Determine whether and where you will change gears. All this is provisional and may get changed a bit when you find out how the course drives.

Some people take a clipboard, pad of paper and pen, and map the course. This is a good procedure. By having to draw the course, you will become more aware of all of the tricky aspects. You will also have something to refer to when you begin to question the wisdom of some of the approaches you are taking, or want to discuss the course with someone else. It is especially important to draw the course if it is not chalk lined. Practices vary around the country, but many clubs do not routinely mark the edges of the course with a chalk line. In these cases you will have to study the map enough to be sure that you know where the course goes and will be able to drive aggressively without spending a lot of time trying to remember the exact path you need to take.

If there is a slalom (see glossary), you should pace off the distance between the pylons. Your driving approach must be based on careful consideration of any differences in distance between the pylons of a slalom.

A few words about motivation: while checking out the course, try to stay out of the mode of deciding that you like or dislike a course. Unless you feel there are serious safety issues with the course, it is simply a challenge of your driving skill

compared to the driving skills of the other
drivers in your class. Sure, there are fast
courses with swooping sweepers and lots of
chance to get your car settled into high-speed

> *All courses offer
> challenges to all drivers*

drifts. You may love these courses a lot. Or, maybe your car is happier on the
tight twisty courses where it can dart around and make you look like a world-
class driver, and you will love <u>these</u> courses. Part of the fun of autocrossing is
seeing how well you can meet a variety of challenges, and you will miss this fun
if you decide from the outset that you don't like a course and let this decision
affect your mood.

6. Drivers' Meeting: Many events include a brief meeting in the morning.
Don't skip this. The people who speak may have announcements of a general
nature, some specific rules to discuss, or they may clarify some specific
requirements of the course. This is a good chance to get specific information if
you need it. You may not want to ask your question during the meeting, but you
can probably figure out who you might approach afterwards.

7. Once the Event Starts: Until you have to be on grid you have a chance to
watch the other drivers on
course. See what lines they are
taking, what seems to be

> *Watch the other drivers on course*

working and what is not working. Watch especially for turns where many
people are spinning. You will want to test those turns on your practice lap (if
any), to see what the turn wants from you and your car.

This is also the time to start running the course in your mind, over and over.
Walk yourself through all the things
you will have to do on the course. If
you do this part well, you can be just a

> *Run the course in your mind*

bit more relaxed on your first run, as you will have, in some sense, already run
the course. That doesn't mean that you should relax, just that this mental pre-
running will give you additional confidence.

8. Getting On Grid: Once grid opens for your run group, get your car onto grid.
While you are on grid, and before your group begins to run, the gridworker will
collect the registration cards and take them to the timing area.

Leave the keys in the car and the car unlocked. No one will steal your car, and
no one will start it without your permission, but people may need to push it to a
slightly different spot if you aren't around to move it. You don't want to be the
owner of the car that has everyone blocked. Don't even consider setting the

alarm. Once your grid group starts moving you will need to pay attention to your car to see if it needs to move forward in the line. If it is a light car, you can move it just by pushing it.

Unless there are some very special circumstances, such as an impending thunderstorm, you want to run as late as you can. There are three reasons for this. First, the cars running the course tend to clean off the grit and debris, so the course gets better all the time. The cars also leave a thin trace of tire rubber in all the right spots (if the drivers are driving a line you like.) The rubber helps make the course sticky. Finally, if you run last, you know what your competitors' times are, so you know how fast you have to go to win, or to move up a place or two. When you are scheduled to run AFTER a competitor in your class, it is called 'having the hammer.'

The nature of the advantage of running after your competitor is that it helps you determine your approach to your next run. If you are just a little behind, and your best run was not terribly precise, you have to concentrate, do everything right, but not take too many chances on hitting pylons or spinning. However, if you drove pretty well, but you are substantially behind anyway, say a second or so, you have only one choice: push yourself a little harder everywhere on the course, and take some chances; see if the car will actually go that much faster. You won't gain anything by a little improvement, so you have to try for a big gain. This may not work out very well, as you are intentionally taking the risks of overdriving the course (driving more aggressively than is effective), but there is nothing to be lost (unless someone is creeping up from behind and beats you by just a little bit, putting you <u>back</u> a place).

How and when you arrive on grid may affect the order in which you run. In some cases, the cars run in the reverse order from the order in which they arrived on grid. This is common for the first run group of the day, so it becomes an advantage to get onto grid early so the other cars are the ones to get the course dried out and cleaned off. In other cases the cars run in the order in which they arrived on grid, and it may be to your advantage to arrive on grid at the last possible moment, so you do not have to run first.

If you set the parking brake when you put your car on grid, set it <u>very tight</u>. Some people, in the excitement of preparing for a run, will forget to release the parking brake. If it was not set firmly, you may not notice that it is on. If you do this, you will have a slower time and the rear brakes will get very hot. When you set the brake firmly, the car will remind you that the brake is on.

9. <u>Preparing to Run</u>: While you are waiting to run, review the course in your mind. Try to imagine everything you will be doing. Imagine braking firmly at the right spots, early enough to get the throttle back down when you need to.

Imagine coming out of key turns fast. Such mental practice is more precise after you have had at least one run at the course, but can make the difference between an OK run and a good run, even the first time out.

When it is getting close to your time to run, the people running grid will probably let you know, but it is your responsibility to get the car warmed up and yourself ready to run. Be sure your seat is in the right position, and, when there are only one or two cars ahead of you on grid, get your helmet and seatbelt on. Continue to use the

> *At the gate get focused, poised and calm*

time to get mentally ready and to run the course in your mind. Grid personnel will tell you when it is time to move over to the starting gate.

When you get to the gate, the person there will need to know your car number so it can be flagged or radioed to the timing people. They need to know who is running. If you have more than one number on the car (because more than one person is running the car), you have to remember which number is yours and tell the gate person or signal by pointing to the correct number.

While you are waiting to make your run, but before you are the next car to go out, relax, breathe deeply, and clear your mind of everything. This is the time to get focused, poised and calm. Do watch how the flagperson is flagging cars onto the track, so you

> *Once you are the next car to go out, don't take your eyes off the flagperson for any reason*

will be ready for the signals being given.

Once you are the next person to go out onto the course, watch the flagperson very carefully. You must enter the course immediately when you get the green flag. If overlap is being used, any failure to move out promptly may put you in the path of the car which is just finishing, risking seriously bent sheet metal and perhaps personal injury. 'Watch very closely' means this: once you are the next car to go out, you never take your eyes off the flagperson, for any reason.

Once the flagperson points at you with the furled green flag, raise your hand outside the window (showing that you are ready and are paying attention), and leave it there until you are flagged onto the course. That way, the flagperson has a clear sign that you are paying attention and are ready to move out when the green flag is waved. It will also remind you not to

> *Enter the course IMMEDIATELY when you are flagged on*

look away. If you cannot raise your hand out the window and keep it there you must at least wave to signal the flagperson that you are ready. This will be your only option if you are at an event that requires you to run with your windows up, as you don't want to be driving out onto the course and rolling up your window at the same time. When the furled green flag is pointed at you, you should also depress the clutch and get the car into first gear, ready to go.

10. Making Your Run: When you are flagged onto the course, move out sharply. If the overlap system is being used, there is another car on the course, and the sooner you get past start/finish and the exit lane, the sooner you will be out of the way of that car. Except for some very specialized autocross formats, such as SCCA Pro-Solo and CMC events, a drag-strip start (maximum acceleration) is not required, and is hard on the car; additionally, if there is another car behind you, you run the risk that your spinning rear tires will spray gravel onto the front of that car, a most anti-social act. Just get moving quickly. If you are running Pro-Solo, you need to have practiced quick, high-rev starts without burning up your clutch; when your lights turn green, you are on the clock, being timed.

Once you enter the course for a run you must complete the run without stopping or leaving the course. If you have a mechanical problem or leave the course voluntarily, you will not get a re-run. If you get off course involuntarily, you must return to the course at the point where you left it.

If you see a red flag being waved while you are on course, come to an immediate and safe stop and await instructions from a courseworker. You will get a re-run. Slowly exit the course and return to the gate area. At some events you will simply get another run. Other clubs carry forward any

> *If you see a red flag, <u>immediately</u> come to a safe and complete stop*

pylons knocked over before you were red flagged. If the pylons are carried forward, you may or may not be assessed additional penalties for hitting the same number of pylons again. If you do not see a red flag, you will eventually see the flagperson waving a checkered flag. This means that your run is over and you should exit safely.

If you get a practice lap, be aggressive. Use it to test ideas about what the course wants and will tolerate. There is no penalty for spins or pylons on the practice lap. However, you may find that a spin on the practice lap is so disorienting that is will affect your concentration during the timed part of your run. Be ready to adjust the plans you made during the coursewalk (or during your previous run) and incorporate changes into your first

> *Use the practice lap to test ideas about what the course wants and will tolerate*

timed lap. Later in the day you should be making only very small adjustments, and the practice lap should be merely a chance to get into the flow and rhythm of the course before the clocks are turned on.

You do have one particular responsibility during the first lap. If you see a pylon down, or out of position (actually, you will rarely be able to see if the pylon is out of position unless it is also knocked over), you need to stop your car by the offending pylon, and wait for a course worker to come over and correct the pylon. Then exit the course. You will be given an official re-run. You may also stop if you see a condition you think unsafe (such as a courseworker running across the course in front of you); be sure you come to a complete stop and discuss the situation with the courseworker; otherwise the flagperson may not realize that you must be given another practice lap or a re-run.

If this is not your first run, and you have been having problems getting the car exactly where you want it, try driving the course at reduced throttle (say, three-quarters) and reduced speed, putting the car exactly where you want it. Then, as you near start/finish, pick up the pace and go for it. This is not a good approach the first time out, when you need to adjust the ideas you gained from the coursewalk to match what the course actually feels like when driven. This is a special approach for those times when you are having trouble doing what you want to do.

You want to be aggressive on the timed laps. For many drivers, there is a surprisingly large difference in time between a 'safe' run and an aggressive one. To be fast you have to be in control at all times, but just barely. It is a delicate balance, and it becomes a lot of fun as you get good at staying on the fine edge.

Anytime there is another car on the course, you must not stop for any reason except a severe emergency. You don't want to be parked in the track when that car comes around. The actual danger is negligible, since the course workers will red flag the other car and the driver may well see you anyway. Nevertheless, do not voluntarily stop unless <u>you</u> are red-flagged or you see a serious condition.

Near the start/finish line, you need to be <u>especially</u> careful to control any inadvertent spins or slides as quickly as possible. There will be spectators, not all of whom are watching what you are doing, and you want to stay well clear of them. You also don't want to run over the timing equipment; it's bad for your car, very bad for the timing equipment and tends to have a decidedly negative impact on your interpersonal relations with the club that owns the timing gear. Again, whenever you see a situation that you do not believe is safe, stop the car.

If you spin the car, immediately press down firmly on the clutch and the brake. You push the clutch down to keep the motor running and avoid letting the tires force the motor to turn backwards when the car is going backwards. The motor will appreciate your concern. You

> *If you spin, immediately push down on the clutch and the brake*

press down on the brakes to stop the car. Do not just let the car decide where it will end up. If you continue off course far enough your fender may encounter an immovable object, such as a light pole or fence, or a movable one such as a courseworker. Autocross courses are designed to be safe, but you must strive to stay on course and, if you are off course, you must stop the car immediately. [If you do spin dramatically, take solace in the quote from the famous economist, John Kenneth Galbraith: "If all else fails, immortality can always be assured by spectacular error."]

At the end of your run, be sure not to let up on the throttle (course conditions permitting) until you have passed the timing equipment at the start/finish line.

11. Leaving the Course: Once you have passed the checkered flag, back off on the throttle, exit safely and drive very slowly over to where timing slips are being handed out. Rules vary, but under most conditions you will be charged for any pylons knocked down, even after start/finish. Don't hit any. As you pull off the course there will be a place to stop to get your timing slip. The timing slip will show you your time for the run (scratch time), any pylon penalty (if any of those pylons just happened to jump out in front of you, or fall over without provocation as you drove by), and a total score (corrected time). It may also show the split time (time for the first lap) if the run consists of two or more timed laps. In most cases the slip is not an official document. Your official score will be posted on a sheet, transcribed from your registration form. It is good practice to check the posted time to be sure that it agrees with the slip you were given. If it does not, you need to find out what has gone amiss. If there was some problem with the course or the timer during your run you will be given an official re-run. In this case you will be directed to proceed over to the starting gate.

```
┌─────────────────────────────┐
│                             │
│      Timing Slip            │
│                             │
│                             │
│      Car #  _____          │
│                             │
│                             │
│   Split Time:  _____     │
│                             │
│   Scratch Time: _____      │
│                             │
│   Pylon Penalty: ____       │
│                             │
│                             │
│   Total Time: _____      │
│                             │
└─────────────────────────────┘
```

1 Timing Slip

Drive very slowly in the pit area. After all the excitement of making a run, it is very easy to continue driving at speeds that are too high for areas where people are walking around. One way to remind yourself to do the right thing is this: once you are completely off the course, bring the car to a complete stop. Then proceed slowly to get your timing slip.

Once you have your timing slip you may spend a moment or two celebrating or

┌─────────────────────────────────────┐
│ *Drive slowly in the pit area*   │
└─────────────────────────────────────┘

moping depending on the quality of your run and your mental condition. If you have another run coming, and you will be the next person to drive the car, return to your previous line on grid to await that run. If someone else will drive the car, you probably need to go to a second-driver line. When you have (temporarily) parked your car, check the tires and adjust the pressure if needed. Also check your fuel level to be sure that you have enough for the next run.

If the grid is on a flat surface, it is best to park the car in gear without setting the parking brake. The brakes will be hot and they will cool better if the pads/shoes are not forced tightly up against the rotors/drums. Of course, not using the parking brakes makes it essential that you are in the habit of starting the car with the clutch disengaged (pushed down).

If you are now finished running, park your car where you unloaded and reload your car. Get ready to work if you signed up for a work session after your run session.

12. Between Your Runs: Analyze your runs. Decide what worked well, and what you want to do differently. Determine which parts of the course are straightforward and don't need much further attention, which parts are challenging but working well, and which parts you are really going to have to improve. If you are taking instruction, talk

> *Most drivers will be happy to share their thoughts about the course*

to your instructor, even if you made this run on your own. If you are having a particular problem, ask an instructor to watch your next run. Talk to other drivers. The situation may be quite competitive, but most drivers will graciously share with you what they think they have learned about the track. Don't be too proud to take advantage of this learning opportunity. As a practical matter, once you become a competent and competitive driver you should not expect a lot of help from the people in your class that you are trying to beat, but some drivers may begin asking to hear your views about the course or driving techniques.

13. Split-time Calculations: When a run consists of two or more timed laps, look at the split time and do some calculating. Find out which lap was the fastest, and by how much. Let's say you had a split time of 36.538 seconds, and a total time of 1:12.120 (or 72.120 seconds.) First, multiply your split time (first lap time) by two (73.076). This is the time you would have if you had run both laps the way you ran the first lap. Now subtract your total time (72.120) from your doubled first-lap time (73.076). You get about a full second (.956 seconds, but few people would ever try to figure it that close in their heads). You now know that your second lap was about a second faster than your first lap, or about 35.6 seconds. Therefore, if you had run both laps as fast as your <u>second</u> lap, you

would have saved about a second. This means that
your total time could have been about one second
less. In this case you clearly <u>could</u> have turned
about 71.2 seconds, without changing anything
except that you drive <u>both</u> laps the way you drove
the second lap.

```
Split time      36.54

2 x split       73.08

Actual time     72.12

Second lap faster
        by        .96

Second lap      35.60

Potential total
      time       71.2
```

Once you have taken the trouble to go through this
calculation you have a target for yourself; there is
no reason you can't turn the 71-second run, since
you have already shown that you can go that
quickly one lap at a time. Try to understand the
differences between the two laps so you know
which approaches are giving you the better times.

2 *Split-time Calculation*

14. At the End of the Day: If you are at the track at the end of the day, help
pick up the course. The work has to be done, and everyone at the event is a
volunteer. It is not complex work; it simply
consists of getting the pylons stacked so they
can be stored away conveniently in a trailer or

Help pick up the course

a van, and putting away the timing equipment, the public address system, any
tables, chairs or awnings that have been set up, etc. If you haven't yet had time
to pack up your car, do it after picking up the course.

Many clubs have a tradition of gathering after an autocross for pizza and beer. If
this is such an event, try to arrange your schedule so you have a chance to attend.
Like you, the people there have spent their day trying to go as fast as possible on
the course. They share your passion for cars and driving. They will have helpful
ideas about driving cars and probably be pretty good company on other
dimensions as well.

15. Various Schedules for Running an Autocross: Operating an autocross
requires both drivers and workers whenever anyone is running the course.
Therefore, various schedules are used to divide the running time and the working
time.

● Two Run Groups: The drivers may be divided into two groups. One group of
drivers takes two to four tries at the course while the other group works the
course. Then the groups switch, with the group that was working now doing the
driving, and vice-versa. This approach is often used in small-club events.

● Three Run Groups: In this approach one group runs, the next works and the
third group rests. Groups are rotated every hour or two.

● Four and Eight Run Groups: These approaches allow people to autocross without spending the entire day at the course. Each car class is assigned to one of the run sessions during the day. Each session lasts one or two hours. People work before or after their session. In the eight-group approach they will work either two groups before or after they run. The run group between is either used to put the car away (when working after running), or is used to get the car ready to run. Any given participant must be at the course for only four hours or so. There is normally a lunch-break/course-walk.

These formats offer one particular advantage in addition to allowing the drivers a part of the day off. Since everyone in a given car class will be running at the same time, everyone in the class gets about the same track surface to run on. In other formats, you may find yourself in a situation where your competition ran mid-morning on a dry track, and you are busy trying to better their time while running during a thunderstorm. Such situations do not usually end up with you receiving the first place trophy.

● Single Run Group: A different approach is simply to cycle all cars through the course on a continual basis throughout the day. Cars are numbered sequentially as they register, and cars run, in order, continually during the event. This approach produces both the most runs for the competitors since very little course time is lost to the time required to change worker crews (ideally no time is lost) and it offers the most even distribution of runs.

In the single run group approach, it is not uncommon for a driver to need to be in two places at once, since the cycling of the grid frequently creates a situation where the next person who is supposed to drive is currently working. This is handled in one of three ways: 1) by assigning some worker positions to be relief workers for those who must drive, 2) by expecting workers to call out to friends to relieve them for a few minutes while they run (this system works best at an event where people know each other pretty well and are reasonably willing to help out as needed), or 3) have people who are working assure that their cars are not blocking any grid lines and wait until their work shifts are over to run (using the second driver line).

16. Course Design & Practice Laps: You won't always get a practice lap. Even on a closed (complete loop) course, some clubs simply decide that they would rather run all laps on the clock than provide any practice laps. Such runs are called 'hot laps'. There may be one hot lap, or two. This saves time and means that each entrant will get an extra run or two at the course.

A different course design is used where the starting and finishing points are not the same place. Since cars are not cycling around the course, it becomes possible to have two or three cars on course at the same time, while still maintaining a safe distance between the cars. This requires somewhat more elaborate timing equipment, as timing lights at both the start line

> *It becomes possible to have three cars on the course at once*

and the finish line will have to trigger the timer. The timing equipment also has to keep track of more than one car. This approach provides a maximum number of runs to competitors. By definition, all runs on these courses are hot laps.

The pressure on the driver is increased when there is just one hot lap. There is no time to get into the rhythm of the course, or get the tires or brakes warmed up. The first time out you simply have to go with your best guess about how well your car will stick.

17. Pro-Solo: There is one established competitive series that uses a format that is very different and very interesting. This is the SCCA Pro-Solo series. It currently consists of about 12 two-day events per year, held around the country. The finals are held in Salina, Kansas each summer, the week after the SCCA Solo II Nationals. CMC, a relative newcomer, is using a similar format for their national series.

At Pro-Solo events you will find two courses of the start-here, finish-there variety. They run parallel to each other, are about 45 seconds long and are mirror images of each other. During the competition there will be cars on both courses at the same time. Indeed, during the first day and a half the two cars will

> *Pro-Solo involves head-to-head competition, safely*

start their runs at exactly the same time, using drag-strip style timing lights. Since the cars are running against each other, there is a spirit of immediate head-to-head competition not usually found in autocrossing. Where the courses point at each other, you can see how your competitor is doing against you.

Entry fees are much higher than for a normal autocross, but each driver gets at least twelve runs, six on each course, so the cost per run is not exorbitant. Additionally, there are significant cash prizes for winning, along with a lot of contingency money from sponsors.

Saturday morning is used for practice sessions (4 runs each driver). Saturday afternoon and Sunday morning are the qualification sessions (4 runs each driver during each of the two sessions).

Sunday afternoon the top two drivers (combined best times on each course) in each of the 15 or so classes compete in the Handicap Challenge runoff. To even things out, since the cars have very different performance potential, the starting lights for each car in the handicap challenge are offset by the difference in the drivers' times during the qualification sessions. So, a stock Mazda 323 would get a large lead over, say, a highly modified Corvette. The Corvette simply has to wait at the signal lights while the Mazda motors on down the track. Finally the Corvette gets the green light and has to try to make up the difference.

This is a fun event. Once you have a little experience in autocrossing, you should consider trying one in your area.

C. Driving Basics

He noticed, as he prepared for the hairpin turn, that he was modulating the brakes, rather than using them fully. Clearly the braking point was too early, and he should simply stay on the throttle longer, then brake harder. The next lap he tries this, and finds that he has applied the brakes much too late, is unable to slow the car in time, and scatters cones everywhere. The next time around he puts the braking point right back where it was originally, and resolves to make such changes in smaller increments in the future.

The three chapters on driving techniques (this chapter, along with the next two), will prepare you to learn the skills needed for good control of your car at the limits of the car's performance. The key word here is PREPARE. You will not learn fast driving from any book. You will learn how to drive your car at its limits from experience. However, to learn as much as you can from your experience, you need to have clear ideas about what you need to do with the car.

This chapter covers the basics; seating position, hand control, use of the throttle and the brakes and dealing with sliding. It also introduces the terms understeer and oversteer and discusses how to control them. The next chapter covers turns, starting with the basic concepts of entry, apex and exit, and discusses the special approaches needed for special types of turns. It also covers heel-and-toe shifting. The final chapter on driving techniques discusses how to analyze a course and determine an entire lap.

Remember, what is unclear at first will, in time, become second nature. Some of this stuff is actually a lot easier to do than to describe. In each chapter you will find basic ideas that you can apply the next time you drive any car, along with advanced concepts that, in some cases, take years to perfect. After reading this section the first time, just use the concepts that make sense to you so far. If you re-read this section of the book after your first autocross school or after you have attended a few autocrosses, then things will begin to gel in your mind a little bit more. Read it again in a few months and you will be pleased by how natural the concepts seem, those same concepts that were so strange a short time ago.

1. Fast is different: The novice driver usually finds that going fast around a
course is quite different from what they expected. Many people come to their
first event thinking that they are already expert drivers. Almost all of them soon
find out there is a lot of difference
between the usual street skills of a good

> *Much of the "fast driving"
> on TV and in the movies is
> not fast at all, just flashy*

driver and true precision driving. Putting
the pedal down hard enough to violate
seriously the national speed laws, and
taking corners with the rear of the car sliding around are certainly insufficient
driving skills, but the issue is deeper than that. The process of learning what you
and your car really can do will involve you at a level of concentration and
coordination that is unlike anything normally needed for street driving.

One of the differences is that things happen extremely fast. It takes some time to
get used to thinking that fast in a vehicle. Particularly in autocrossing, the turns
come at you quite quickly. By

> *In autocross you are facing turns
> FOUR TIMES AS OFTEN as a
> formula-car driver turning a
> record lap on a roadrace course*

way of comparison, the turns are
linked together so closely at an
autocross that you are facing turns
four times as often as a formula-car
driver turning a record lap at a
roadracing course such as Lime Rock. You are not going four times as fast, just
negotiating corners much more often. Another difference is that much of the
'fast driving' on TV and in the movies is not fast at all, just flashy. So you have
to unlearn some preconceptions. Your new perceptions will become automatic
with practice.

2. The Learning Process: The process of learning to drive well involves practice.
Find a fast and controlled driver at an event and you will find someone who has
been doing this for awhile. If you enjoy the sport, then you won't need any
encouragement about practicing. You will find yourself, like the rest of us,
getting up at indecently early hours on weekend days, driving longish distances,
fiddling with tire pressures and doing all the other things needed to get some
track time and to be competitive. On the other hand, if you only come out for
one or two events a year, you will still learn, but at a much slower rate. There is
no substitute for time on course. However, coming out for even a small number
of autocrosses will certainly help make you a better driver overall.

Watching fast drivers is also a key part of the learning process. From a safe
vantage point well inside the course, watch the drivers who are doing well. See
where they use the brakes, and how hard they are braking. Watch the lines they
take through turns. See if they are using throttle or brakes to turn the car. See
how slowly they go through slow turns. Listen to the motor to see how much
throttle they are feeding in at various points. You will learn a lot.

At most events there will be instruction available. Don't be too proud to ask for instructors as long as you think you have something to learn. You will have plenty to learn for the first ten years or so. It is not uncommon to find drivers who are dominating their classes, still taking instructors out from time to time to see what they

> *Don't be too proud to ask for instruction as long as you think you have something to learn*

might do better. Also, if you can arrange it, try to get a ride with a very good driver who is driving a car similar to yours. This will be difficult to do if the event is structured so each driver gets just a very few runs, as the other driver will not want your extra weight in the car. At non-points events, or at events where everyone will get many runs, most drivers will consider taking a passenger occasionally. Rules about passengers vary. One of the people in the car will probably have to be a qualified instructor. The person you want to ride with probably is an instructor anyway.

Learning to drive well involves a certain level of humility. It is silly ever to think that you are driving so well that your times are strictly limited by the car. You will hear some drivers saying that they are going as fast as the car will go, and there is nothing left to do. This is always dead wrong. There are always ways to do better. Stay open to finding ways to improve your driving. If you don't think the car will go any faster, just put an expert in the driver's seat and see how much faster it will go.

Concentration is the most essential skill needed for competitive driving. You need to prepare yourself mentally before you run. You need to be able to deal with everything that is happening while you are on the course. Afterwards, you need to sit quietly for a moment, review the run, and determine what happened, why, and what you

> *Concentration is your most important skill*

might do differently next time. Sometimes you will have the delightful opportunity to be able to sit and ponder what you know to be an absolutely excellent run; at those times you need to review all the things you did right to see how you can do this well all the time.

Success in any sport involves determination. This is partially your decision, in that you may determine that you want to be a fast driver. It is also God's decision, not your own, whether or not you are truly interested in this sport. If you find yourself interested, you need to be patient with yourself during those times when you don't seem to be improving. Learning comes in stages,

> *By gradual and deliberate changes, you will steadily approach the maximum potential of you and your car*

and it is quite normal to continue for some time at a certain level, trying your best to improve and seeing precious little in the way of results, then suddenly finding yourself having attained a whole new plateau. Sometimes the learning is going on underneath at a pretty steady rate, but surfaces in batches. Be patient with yourself and practice, practice, practice.

The learning process also involves having the patience to make small changes, and determine their effect before making other changes. Once you have got a good sense of the basics of competitive driving, you will be unlikely to make progress by trying to improve by leaps and bounds in a single run. Rather, you need to try to move that braking point by just a few feet, close the distance between the car and the apex pylon from 8 inches to 3 inches, or get the slip angle more precise. By such gradual and deliberate changes you will steadily approach the maximum potential of you and your car.

3. Seating Position: The way your body fits into the car, and the way you use your hands and feet are both important to driving effectively. You touch the car through your hands, your feet, and your entire seating position. It is important that these be right, and that you are confident that they are right, so you and your car can become a single, highly-tuned unit.

You should sit so you have excellent access to the throttle pedal, brake pedal and clutch. It may be that the seat will be a little more forward than you use for normal street driving. The seat back should be relatively upright, so you have an excellent view of the road and can easily reach the steering wheel. You need some bend in your arms so you can comfortably keep your hands on the wheel while you are turning it. Be sure that you can easily reach the gear shift lever.

If your car seat is low slung, don't be afraid to use an extra cushion to get your eyes up to the level needed. In some cars you will already be sitting too high and may wish to remove the bottom cushion or replace it with one that is thinner. If you are unsure of how high you want to sit, err on the side of sitting too high. You will have a better view of the nose of the car and of the track, and will feel a little less lost in the interior of the car.

Do whatever you need to help you keep from being thrown sideways when the car is cornering at its maximum potential. If your car has four-point seat belts (lap belt and two shoulder harnesses), wear them. They will tend to keep you solidly in the seat, allowing you to focus your attention on driving. Turner [see bibliography] notes that you can make the normal inertial-reel belts hold you more firmly, by twisting the part that plugs in a couple of turns before plugging it in. Be sure that you have the plug-in part at the right point along the belt before doing the twisting.

If you can find a solid resting place for your left foot and press down

> **Find a place to rest your left foot**

firmly, you will notice that this tends to force your butt solidly into the seat. Doing this while driving will help you remain stable in your seat. It will therefore also help you avoid grabbing the steering wheel tightly, which some people do to try to maintain their position in the seat when cornering aggressively. You want to have 'light hands' as much as possible. Try to drive with some pressure on the left foot (unless you have to use it for the clutch or for left-foot braking). It takes a bit of practice to keep some tension in that left leg without letting your whole body get tense, but it can be done.

4. Hand Position on the Steering Wheel: This is a tricky topic and there are a variety of approaches. This section covers general guidelines along with two specific methods for handling very sharp turns.

First, drive with <u>both</u> hands. Do not drive around with one hand resting on the gearshift. Your hand needs to be on the gearshift only when you are changing gears. Nor should you have one elbow resting on the window sill, with the fingers lightly trying to steer the car. Both hands are needed firmly on the wheel.

3 Normal Hand Position

Your hands normally should be at the sides of the steering wheel with your thumbs wrapped around the wheel just above, and resting on, the horizontal wheel spokes. By reference to a clock face, your hands are at 9:00 and 3:00. Your grip should be comfortable. It is not uncommon for drivers to maintain a death grip on the steering wheel while driving the course. The death grip will tire you unnecessarily and is a poor method. Practice a firm but comfortable grip. One good exercise is to remind yourself, occasionally, to leave your hand on the wheel and wiggle your fingers just a bit. This will interrupt the death grip.

<u>Never</u> grab the steering wheel from the inside, or grab the spokes of the steering wheel. You risk twisting your wrist (as well as losing control of the car!) when you

> *Never grab the wheel from the inside*

have to move the steering wheel. Always grab the wheel from the outside.

You should not reposition your hands any more than is necessary. In particular, you want to avoid constantly shifting your hands around on the steering wheel. Just leave them where they are, and turn your hands and the wheel together (as one unit) as far as you can. As you exit the turn simply rotate the steering wheel back to its center position, maintaining a firm grip on the wheel.

If you have enough arm strength and let your wrists flex a bit you may find that you can allow your forearms to cross (both thumbs pointing relatively downward), turning the steering wheel a complete 180°. You should try this, but don't worry if you can't turn the wheel that far. There always will be turns that require

> *You should not reposition your hands on the steering wheel any more than absolutely necessary*

more steering wheel movement than you can accomplish while leaving your hands in place; we'll deal with that in section 4a. To test how far you can turn the wheel while leaving your hands in place, you need to have the car moving. Ten MPH is sufficient. Do this on an empty parking lot, or some place where you will not pose a danger to people or property while you are concentrating more on the steering wheel and less on where you are going!

Do not let the steering wheel slip through your hands while exiting a turn; you won't have the control necessary to make slight corrections that are needed when you power out of the turn with full throttle. Some cars have a very strong centering force. That is, when the car is in motion the steering wheel will try very hard to return itself to the center position. Because of this, some people

> *Do not let the steering wheel slip through your hands*

have found that, as they exit a turn, they can release their grip on the steering wheel and let the wheel slip through their fingers until the tires are pointed straight ahead, then re-grip the wheel at the 9:00 and 3:00 points. Some respected drivers actually do this, but most of them do not advocate it as a technique, and this is not the reason they are respected. If you really let go of the steering wheel, you may or may not re-grab it at exactly the right spots (9:00 & 3:00). If you don't get the right spots, you will have to futz around a bit to get your hands where you want them. Even if you don't let go completely, you still have judgments to make about when to re-grab the wheel.

Some people place a piece of brightly colored tape at the 12:00 position on the steering wheel, so, when things get a little out of control, they know where to put the steering wheel to get the tires pointed straight ahead. This should not be necessary if you have good discipline with your hands and never let go of the steering wheel. Further, if you are in the midst of desperately trying to regain control of the direction of the car, when, pray, are you going to have time to look at the tape?

4a. Moving Your Hands: There are two basic methods available for those turns where you must move your hands. Either one will feel a bit strange at first. It is very important that you select an approach you like and PRACTICE IT BEFORE YOU DRIVE AT A COMPETITIVE EVENT. Both techniques take practice to become automatic. Once you are on the course it is too late to start thinking about hand position; you will have many other things to think about. Take the book, go sit in the car, and try it out.

The Shifty-Hand Method (as advocated by Donohue, Bondurant and Mitchell). The first method is to prepare for tight turns by shifting the hand position ahead of time. The hands (one at a time) are moved around the steering wheel as much as needed before entering the turn. You then can execute the

Practice hand control BEFORE you autocross or time trial

turn without moving your hands around on the steering wheel during the turn. This is a good advantage. In some cases you may have to shift your hands more than once.

The disadvantage of this method is related to needing to correct for a spin or for some drifting of the car. If you have moved your hands on the steering wheel, you will have to remember the position to which you must bring them to have the tires pointed straight ahead again. On a long-term basis this may be the best approach, and is probably the better time trial approach, but only if you will remember which hands-on-the-steering-wheel position points the tires straight-ahead when all hell breaks loose.

Even using this method you should be able to turn the steering wheel a substantial amount without repositioning your hands. The repositioning is only for those turns where simply turning the wheel is not enough.

Per the accompanying illustration (and based on a turn to the left), the steps for this method are:

a. You are driving with your hands in their normal position, but you are approaching a turn that will require you to shift your hands.

b. You move one hand to a new position. This can be either hand, but what is illustrated is the 'hand over' variation. In this case, for a left turn, move the left hand around the top of the steering wheel until it is near the right hand. Grab the steering wheel with the left hand.

c. Move the right hand to the bottom of the steering wheel, and grasp the wheel.

Note: Steps b & c can also be accomplished by moving the right hand to the bottom of the wheel first, then moving the left hand.

d. Turn the wheel as needed to negotiate the turn. Your hands will be relatively horizontal and you will have good control of the car.

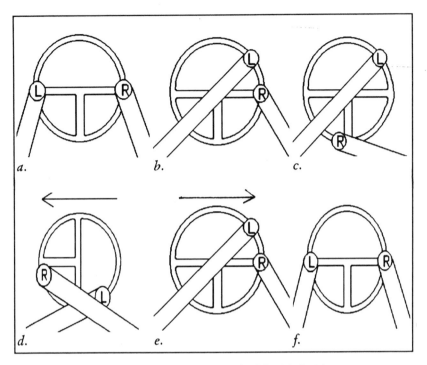

4. The Shifty Hands Pre-positioning Method for Tight Turns

e. As you exit the turn, and are moving the steering wheel back to its center position, move the right hand back to its normal position by the right spoke.

f. After you have grasped the wheel with the right hand, move the left hand back to its normal position.

Note: Steps e & f can also be accomplished by moving the left hand first, then moving the right hand.

If your car requires many turns of the steering wheel to get the front tires turned sufficiently, then the Shifty Hands method will be your only choice. Such steering is common on front-wheel

> *Cars with slow steering may require you to reposition your hands several times*

drive cars, and on some cars that were not designed with competitive driving in mind. In these cars, you may need to adjust your hands two or three times turning into the turn, and similarly coming out of the turn.

The <u>Zaccone Method</u>. The second method leaves one of your hands in the same position on the steering wheel during any turn. The other hand may be shifted around to provide extra muscle power to turn the wheel.

The advantage of this approach is that, when you get the car into a serious spin, you can immediately know where the tires are pointed by the position of the hand that did not move. You have one less thing to think about, as you know instinctively what you must do to get the front tires

> *The second method leaves ONE of your hands in exactly the same place on the steering wheel during any turn*

pointed straight ahead. This is a good advantage and is the approach favored by this author. Additionally, it seems a more effective approach for the extremely rapid steering input required when autocrossing. However, this method does require good arm strength, and will be unsuitable for people unable to turn the steering wheel 180° without repositioning their hands. It will also be more difficult, or perhaps infeasible, on cars that require a great deal of steering wheel turning to turn the front tires.

Note that the advantage is probably not in faster lap times. Both methods, properly executed, should be about equal in lap times. The advantage of this method lies in having better control of the car when things are getting out of control. If you are a very aggressive driver on the track (as Zaccone is), the Zaccone hand method is something you should seriously consider.

Per the accompanying illustration (and based on a turn to the left), the steps for this method are:

a. You are driving the course with your hands in their normal position.

b. You enter a turn that is very tight. You turn the wheel 180° and determine that this is not enough.

c. Let go of the wheel with your left hand, and bring it over the top of your right arm, grabbing the wheel at about the 1:00 position.

d. Continue to turn the wheel. Relax the grip with the fingers of your right hand, but <u>keep your right thumb in place on the steering wheel, in the intersection of the steering wheel and the spoke</u>.

e. As you exit the turn you begin turning the steering wheel back toward center. It will come back to the point at which you originally moved your left hand.

g. At this point release your grip with your left hand and move it back to its normal position. Continue turning the steering wheel as you exit the turn until the wheel is back to its centered position.

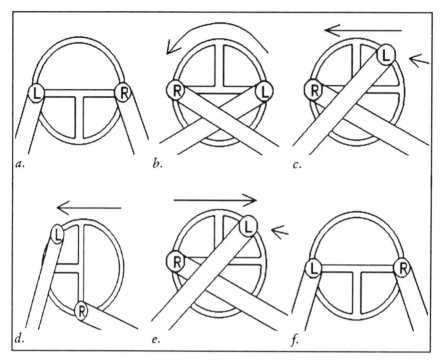

5. Zaccone Fixed-hand Method for Tight Turns

<u>5. Gas (Throttle)</u>: When throttle is called for you should use it with great vigor. Except specific cases where the throttle must be used gently, when it comes time to push down on the throttle, smoothly push it ALL THE WAY DOWN. You will not hurt a car that is in good shape and has been adequately maintained. Hundreds of thousands of engineering man-hours (people-hours?) have been spent to make

> **When throttle is called for, use it with great vigor**

sure that your car is not only ready for this, but will actually seem to enjoy it. The cases where you must be gentle with the throttle will be covered in more detail later, but they include a few specific maneuvers (such as a long, constant radius turn), and when driving cars that have a great deal of horsepower and not very much traction.

Make a smooth transition from throttle-off to throttle-on, rather than abruptly jamming the throttle. If your car has a great deal of power, or the course surface does not have very much traction, you may have to allow a second or so to change from no throttle to full throttle. You may also have to adjust (modulate) the throttle as you go along to keep the wheels just short of spinning. One sign that you are making the transition too abruptly or applying too much throttle altogether is finding that the rear wheels have started to spin. If this happens in a turn, the entire car will also start to spin.

<u>6. Braking</u>: Braking is extremely important to precision driving, and you must brake well to achieve good lap times. In roadracing, more passes between competitive cars are made under braking than under acceleration. In general, if you are not using the throttle with great vigor, you should be using the brakes with great vigor; there is almost <u>never</u> a reason to be coasting. You should either be accelerating as briskly as you can, or braking for all you are worth. Your lap times will improve if you can brake harder for a shorter time, and if you do this at the last possible moment before entering a turn. This is called 'going deep into a turn.'

The transition from throttle to brakes should be made as smoothly as possible You can greatly unsettle the car and overload your suspension and tires by abrupt use of the brakes. How long the transition should take will depend on your car's suspension, but a half second to a second is reasonable to

> *If you are not using the throttle with great vigor, you should be using the brakes with great vigor. Don't coast*

move from no brakes to full braking. This will seem like a very fast transition at first. With practice you will be able to do it <u>too fast</u>; then you will have to become more gentle and let the suspension work for you.

Braking will, in general, happen in a straight line. The reason for this has to do with weight transfer. When you aggressively apply the brakes, weight shifts to the front of the car. However, the mass does not move. So now you have, at the rear of the car, all that mass, but the weight that should be there along with it has moved to the front of the car. This means the front tires are pressing very firmly on the pavement, but the rear tires are not. The feeling to the driver is that the back end has become light. As long as the car is traveling in a <u>very</u> straight line, all is well. However, if the car is in a turn, then the centrifugal force on the rear of the car will overcome the minimal traction of the rear tires, the tires will loose their grip, and the car will begin to spin.

Later, this chapter discusses the sequence of events necessary to get through a turn quickly. For now there is a gentle caution to aggressive drivers: once you have grasped the notion of braking late you

> *After you have learned to brake late enough, learn to brake <u>early</u> enough*

run a strong risk of braking <u>too</u> late. While practicing late braking, be sure to leave time to get back on the gas when you need to. Depending upon the car and the turn, you may need to be on the gas <u>before</u> entering a turn. Exactly when you need to get back on the throttle will depend upon the handling characteristics of your car in this turn and the approach you are taking. In any case, be <u>sure</u> that your late braking is <u>not</u> getting in the way of your getting the throttle back on when you need it. Drivers with just a little bit of experience often make the mistake of braking <u>too</u> late.

Full braking does NOT mean locking up the wheels to the point that they are no longer rotating. The best braking requires a constant subtle adjustment (modulation) of the pedal, to keep the tires very near to locking up but not actually locked up. Wheels that are not turning are nearly useless; you might as well have a bale of rubber lashed to each corner of the car. No matter what you

> *Full braking does NOT mean locking up the wheels*

do with the steering wheel you will have no ability to turn a car that has its wheels locked up.

You will occasionally see some bits of smoke coming from the front tires of cars being autocrossed. Either the driver was over-aggressive with the brakes, or the car is ever so slightly in a turn under hard braking. When the car is turning it is not possible to apply the brakes quite as firmly as when the car is traveling in a straight line. Also, when the car is turning slightly, the inside tire, which is momentarily carrying less weight because the weight has shifted to the outside of the car, will often lock up and emit a puff of smoke. This will also cause a flat spot on the tires, which may be inconsequential, or may cause the car to go BUMP-BUMP-BUMP all the way home.

<u>6a. Trail-Braking</u>: Trail-braking is the process of leaving some brakes on as you begin to enter a turn. This will induce some oversteer (see the next section), and should only be used when you have a reason for the oversteer. In some cases the only point to trail-braking is to get the car slowed down, and it just happens that the car will be turning when it needs to slow, and that the induced oversteer will not unduly unsettle the rear end of the car. In other cases you are actually welcoming the oversteer. If there is a turn that is making your car understeer and you induce some

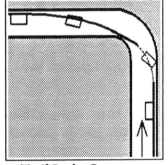

6 Trail Brake Oversteer

oversteer, then natural understeer + your induced oversteer = regular steer, we hope. Or, you may actually be trying to get the back end sliding a bit.

The technique is to continue (but reduce) the application of brakes while you are beginning the turn. If you are using trail-braking to induce sliding at the rear wheels, when the car is pointed the direction you desire, apply the throttle smoothly to transfer weight to the back of the car. This

> *If you get the back end sliding very rapidly, the mere application of a little throttle will make very little difference*

will encourage the rear tires to stop sliding. All this will work quite well, once you can coordinate the brakes and throttle as described, as long as you don't expect magic from the technique. If you get the back end sliding very rapidly you are, by definition, already in a serious spin, and the mere application of a little throttle is unlikely to make much difference.

Trail-braking will, in some cases, suggest a slightly different line, as the car will be more willing to turn. The key is to pick out where you want to be when you begin feeding in throttle, and arrange the braking and oversteer to get to that place pointed the direction you want to point.

Be <u>very</u> <u>careful</u> about using trail-braking at higher speeds. In most cases, the higher the speed, the more trail-braking will induce oversteer. Use this technique <u>only</u> when you have understeer that you wish to neutralize. Be sure that you are <u>not</u> going to be expecting the car to be cornering at its normal limit before you have completed the trail-braking. Also, see friction circles in 7b.

6b. Left-foot and Hand-brake Braking: It is possible to use the left foot on the brakes, or using the hand-brake for certain turns. These are specialized techniques, generally applicable only for certain cars. Left foot braking offers the possibility of slowing the car just slightly, without all the unsettling that happens if you also lift your foot from the throttle. Left foot braking can also be very useful if you are driving a car with a turbocharger. It can be very important to keep turbos on the boost. If you don't have to slow down very much, it may be to your advantage simply to tap the brakes with your left foot, leaving your throttle on. You can actually do quite a bit of braking this way, though there is a limit, of course. Almost all cars will brake better than they will accelerate, so the brakes will overpower the motor. Since the brakes have to do more work (slowing the car and counteracting the power of the engine), they will get hotter.

Hand-brake braking (well, parking-brake braking; sometimes it is a foot-pedal) is a method of inducing quite a bit of oversteer (see 7c), by putting drag only on the rear tires and doing this while they are unweighted. To use hand-brake braking you have to modify the hand-brake so it no longer locks on. For front-wheel drive cars which display a great deal of understeer in slow turns, an application of rear-only brakes can swing the rear end of the car out enough to get the front wheels straight. This makes it possible to apply the throttle earlier, resulting in a faster exit from the turn.

7. Sliding: You may think it strange that sliding is included as a 'driving basic'. While not a beginner's technique, controlled sliding is basic to performance driving and must be understood before other topics can be introduced. You need to understand the way the car behaves when one end or the other is sliding a little bit or a lot. The rest of this chapter will cover the slip angle of the tires (the difference between where the tires are pointed and where they are going), the friction circle (which describes the extent to which we can combine braking and turning - or acceleration and turning), oversteer and understeer, in that order.

The sliding or drifting that helps you achieve fast lap times is nearly imperceptible to the casual observer. It is called 'drifting'. It happens when you drive briskly and precisely and you will soon get used to it. Indeed, you will soon enjoy it a lot. If you carefully watch the drivers

> *If you get used to dramatic, tail-out cornering, you will also get used to slow lap times*

who are winning their classes you will see people who are very smooth, who are not jerking the car around very much and who do not charge through the corners with the tail of the car hanging way out. In spite of the smooth appearance, they are sliding. If you get used to dramatic, tail-out cornering (which is always a crowd-pleaser for sure, nearly as good as a 360° spin), you should also prepare to get used to slow lap times.

7a. Slip Angle: The slip angle for any tire that is not fully sliding is the difference between the direction it is pointed and the direction it is traveling. In the illustration, 'a' is the direction the tire is pointed, 'b' is the direction it is actually traveling, and 'c' is therefore the slip angle. (Once the tire is fully sliding the term slip angle has no further meaning.) The cornering force will increase as the slip angle increases, up to a certain point. If both ends of the car are slipping within a good range, the perceived effect is a gentle crabbing to the side while the car corners. This is called drifting. To achieve this there needs to be a correct

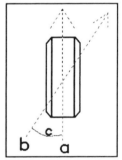

7 Tire Slip Angle

balance between the car and the driving technique. As slip angle increases, the tire also acts to slow the car. This is one of several reasons that the flashiest driving (high slip angles at the rear of the car) is not usually the fastest driving.

The slip angles at both ends of the car are a function of weighting on each corner and the lateral forces on the tire. The weighting is changed by the use of brakes and throttle, shifting weight from one end of the car to the other. The lateral forces are, in turn, a function of the direction the tire is pointed compared to the direction the tire is being pushed. It is worth keeping in mind that the slip angle at the front can be changed almost immediately and fairly precisely by making steering corrections. Changing the rear slip angle may be done through adjustments in throttle, braking and steering, all of which act more slowly on the rear tires than steering operates on the front tires.

8 Drift

While you are on course, you will need to be constantly adjusting the slip angle of the tires, by the entire way in which you handle the car. Too little slip angle, and you aren't using the tire effectively. Too great, and you are creating excess drag on the car. Nikki Lauda writes that cars corner best when this angle is about 10° to 15°, Skip Barber thinks the proper range is 7° to 10°. Your optimum slip angle will depend on several factors. The actual type, brand and size of tire you are using will be

High slip angles slow the car down

very important. Any given tire will have a range in which it will perform best. Also very important is the relative amount of power of your car. If your car is relatively underpowered, you should use lower slip angles, being sure not to trade too much of that hard-earned forward motion for cornering power. If you have power to spare, you can operate at higher slip angles, regaining speed as necessary.

Your path through a turn will be a combination of the slip angles at the front and rear of the car, as well as the direction the front tires are pointed. Once you get good at rapidly loading the suspension, and living with the right amount of slip angle, you will find that you are sometimes pointing the car in what might seem like slightly strange directions. You will approach a corner,

You may be pointing the car in slightly strange directions

turn the car, and find that it looks like it is going to pass <u>inside</u> the apex pylon. The slip angle of the car will carry you just outside the pylon, at the fastest speed you will be able to attain for that turn.

The beginning driver will find it more comfortable to use appropriate slip angles at autocross speeds, and in the safety of an autocross environment. The principles work the same at higher speeds. Even experienced autocrossers, when beginning to time trial, will often drive with almost no slip angle. This is an appropriate way to begin. Once the driver has more experience at time trialing, the sensation of being able to control the drift of a car at higher speeds will develop naturally.

<u>7b.</u> <u>The Friction Circle</u>: Beginning competitive drivers are often told not to brake and turn at the same time. This is good <u>beginning</u> advice. Spins result very quickly when the driver tries to combine too much braking with too much turning. However, a tire doesn't care very much which direction it has to push, as long as it can keep rolling. Therefore, you <u>can</u> combine braking and turning, if you do it right. (A tire's effectiveness decreases enough when locked — roughly 15% to 20% — that you <u>do</u> want to keep it rolling.)

The friction circle is often used to illustrate the <u>extent</u> to which a tire can both brake and turn (or accelerate and turn) at the same time. On the illustration, the horizontal axis represents the amount of cornering a tire will do, and the vertical axis represents how much acceleration or braking is available. Tires may corner more or less than they will brake, depending on details of tire and tread design, and the circle might become a bit elliptical. The point of the circle is this: a tire <u>can</u> brake and corner at the

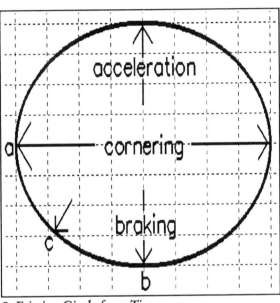

9 *Friction Circle for a Tire*

same time, and the competent driver can therefore balance some braking with some turning. A tire can operate <u>anywhere</u> <u>on</u> or <u>within</u> the circle.

In the drawing shown, maximum cornering is shown at point <u>a</u>, maximum braking at point <u>b</u>, and a combination of braking and cornering at point <u>c</u>. Note that, at point <u>c</u>, one can presumably apply about 70% of the maximum cornering force, and about 70% of the maximum braking force.

> *The CAR friction circle is <u>not</u> the same shape at all speeds*

It is <u>absolutely critical</u> that you not confuse the friction circle for a <u>tire</u>, which is shown in the diagram, with the friction circle of a <u>car</u>. A <u>tire</u> will brake and turn at the same time without difficulty. The extent to which a <u>car</u> can combine braking and turning is dependent on many factors, all of which need to be understood before the driver decides how much braking and turning can happen at the same time. In many cars, during a high-speed turn, simply lifting the

---

throttle will abruptly initiate a spin (indicating that we have exceeded the maximum cornering power of the rear tire), nevermind applying any brakes.

7c. Oversteer: Oversteer is the condition in which you begin a turn and find the back end of the car sliding to the outside of the turn because the rear tires have temporarily lost their grip on life (or at least their grip on the track surface). It is called <u>over</u>steer because, having turned the steering wheel just a bit (to the left, say) , the car is now rotating rather dramatically to the left. Actually, it is the rear of the car moving to the right that is pointing the front of the car to the left.

10 Oversteer

Technically, oversteer is described as a condition in which the slip angle at the rear of the car is greater than the slip angle at the front of the car. The basic causes of oversteer are excessive power applied to the rear wheels, jerking the steering wheel to one side or the other at moderate or high speeds, braking or lifting the throttle during hard cornering, or simply trying to turn the car more than available rear-wheel traction will allow.

Oversteer is greater at higher speeds for essentially all cars except pure race cars. There are two reasons. The first happens as turns increase from very slow to medium in speed, and is related to steering geometry. At very slow speeds, the front wheels will be turned a great deal to negotiate the turn.

> *The tendency of a car to oversteer usually increases with speed*

(If it isn't a sharp turn, requiring quite a bit of wheel-turning, then you wouldn't be going that slow, would you?) When the front wheels are turned sharply, camber changes, in part due to caster. Since the camber was set about where you wanted it, the change is for the worse, and the front tire sticks less well. Since the front tire sticks less well, it requires additional turning to have the desired effect. So, the car <u>understeers</u> more at slow speed. Conversely, you could say it oversteers more at a higher speeds.

The second cause of greater oversteer at higher speeds is more relevant as you move from medium speeds to high speeds, at which point aerodynamics begin to play a stronger role. On the bodies of most cars that were designed for street use, the center of aerodynamic pressure moves forward at greater speeds. This is due to downward pressure at the front of the car and over a sloped windshield, and lift over the roof and at the back of the car. The effect of this is to transfer weight from the back to the front, allowing the front of the car to stick better and the rear of the car to stick less well. This change increases oversteer.

A small amount of oversteer will not be a problem if you don't do anything to make it worse. Just leave the throttle where it is and point the car where you want it to go. Lifting your foot from the throttle or applying brakes will just make the situation worse by transferring the weight to the front and away from the rear of the car. Applying much more throttle may spin the rear tires, further reducing traction at the rear of the car.

To correct a moderate-to-serious oversteer condition you must first stifle your natural tendency to apply the brakes when things are getting a little scary. IF YOU APPLY THE BRAKES, YOU WILL CERTAINLY SPIN THE CAR. If you are applying full throttle and this is the main cause of the problem, you should reduce throttle somewhat. A dramatic reduction of throttle will tend to

> *A small amount of oversteer will not be a problem if you don't do anything to make it worse*

slow the car, transferring weight from the rear of the car to the front of the car, and we already have a condition where there is not enough weight on the rear of the car for the rear tires to get a good grip.

If the main problem is the speed at which you are trying to take the turn, and not the large amount of power you are applying, you will not want to come off the throttle completely. Rather, back off the throttle just a small bit, and point the front tires toward the direction the whole car is traveling. As long as the car is dramatically oversteering your first responsibility is to regain control of the car. Worry about your lap times and the pylons (if you are autocrossing) later. If you are time trialing and have got yourself into a condition of moderate-to-serious oversteer you have made a pretty big mistake and you may well be heading off the road surface soon. Your reactions should be the same, it's just a lot more important that you respond correctly.

In autocrossing, if when you get the car completely sideways, or find yourself in a major spin, your first responsibility is not to panic. Most cars will simply not tip over on relatively flat pavement, no matter what you do to them. Second, and very quickly, put in the clutch and apply the brakes firmly. Keep a firm grip on the steering wheel during all of this. Then wait until the car stops. If you have a car with standard suspension, a

> *Most cars will NOT tip over*

high center of gravity (such as an 'econobox') and competition tires, it is possible that the car might tip over if mishandled. Talk to competitors running the same type of car if you are concerned about this. If it turns out that you have good reason to be afraid of rolling the car, find another car or get the suspension set up for safer handling.

Autocross courses are usually designed so there is adequate runoff room at the points likely to induce sliding and spinning, but some cautions are in order. Due to space limitations, some clubs <u>will</u> set up a course where part of the boundary is a solid object such as fence or a curb. You need to adjust your driving accordingly. If you have lots of runout room, explore the limits of the car and your driving as much as you care to. Where you have very little room, stay completely within your limits.

In time trialing, the effects of going off course are often much more severe. In time trialing you must be <u>sure</u> to stay on course, and drive completely within the limits of the car.

<u>7d. Induced Oversteer</u>: Induced oversteer can be used to great advantage. It allows you to turn the car without slowing down, and without turning the steering wheel very much. Such techniques <u>are</u> a bit tricky and represent a high degree of coordination between a well-balanced car and its driver. Once mastered, they allow you to make surprisingly small corrections in the attitude of the car without losing much speed.

The basics are fairly simple. You can lift partially or completely off the throttle; the engine will try to slow down the rear tires, which will begin to lose their grip, causing them to begin to slide to the outside of the turn, resulting in oversteer. If that is not enough, you may

> *The person who is best at keeping the front tires pointed straight will win*

also add in a little braking to transfer weight to the front of the car, resulting in less grip at the rear, increasing oversteer. Or, you can apply more power than the grip at the rear will handle; once the tires begin to spin, they will also begin to slip to the outside of the turn, resulting in oversteer. Power-on oversteer usually works more effectively in slower corners. It is a little more difficult to control, but can be used if you want to add a little speed at the point you want the oversteer, rather than dropping a little speed.

Oversteer may be induced on front-wheel drive cars by reducing throttle, but the effect is mixed; weight does transfer to the front when the throttle is lifted, but only because the front tires are <u>also</u> being used to slow the car, reducing the amount of traction available for cornering. In some

> *Left-foot braking will induce oversteer in front-wheel drive cars*

turns this may induce a bit of oversteer in some cars. The better approach is to use left-foot braking while leaving the power on. If you do it effectively, the brakes and engine will more or less fight to a draw on the front tires, but the increased drag on the rear tires will decrease grip there and the back end will begin to slide the outside of the turn, causing oversteer.

One effect of throttle steering is that you will be able to keep the front tires of the car pointed relatively straight ahead. From this position they can do their most effective work. It is frequently said that the person who keeps the front tires pointed straight the most will win.

Also, a word of caution is in order. Oversteer can be great fun. Some people, having learned to oversteer their car at interesting speeds, begin to believe that, since the back end is sliding, this must be just about as fast as the car will go. I have seen students happily (and in control) oversteering their

> *Induced oversteer is not __always__ the fastest way around a turn*

cars through sweepers that called for an entirely different approach. Only comparing lap times in the same car could convince them that any other approach would be quicker. Some people will also tend to use oversteer in almost any corner. Once you have learned to control oversteer, be sure you treat it as a technique, not the technique.

7e. Underster (pushing, plowing): Understeer is the name applied to the condition occurring when you try to get the car to turn and find that it just wants to go in a straight line. The term understeer refers to the fact that you have diligently turned the steering wheel enough to get around the turn (well, you might get around the turn if you were going a little slower and weren't

> *Understeer happens when the rear tires are maintaining traction and the front tires are not*

understeering), but the car is turning less than you had hoped and less than the steering input would normally dictate. 'Less steering effect' translates to 'understeering'.

Understeering can have bad effects on your autocross score, because finding that the car is not turning when you want it to turn usually means you are about to assassinate large numbers of pylons; the pylons will have the final revenge, however, by adding 1 second each to your lap time. In some parts of the country they will add two seconds to your time! Understeer will normally happen at time trials only on the slower turns, but, if you don't control it, you may hit more than pylons.

Technically, understeer is the condition in which the slip angle at the front of the car is greater than at the rear of the car. Understeering happens when the rear tires are maintaining traction and the front tires are not. Once the front tires start sliding they will no longer apply force to make the front of the car move to either side, so the car simply goes straight ahead, or whichever direction it was pointed when the tires lost their grip. Like oversteering, understeer is not an all-or-nothing phenomenon. You may feel the front end pushing or washing out just

a little, or you may find that the car is going
absolutely straight ahead even though you have the
steering wheel turned.

Understeer is usually the result of simply trying to
push your car through a lower-speed turn faster than
it can handle. The obvious solution to this is to brake
sooner <u>before</u> the turn. Or, if you are not fully using
the brakes, then brake harder before the turn. If you
are having an understeer problem in a particular turn,
you may want to use some method for inducing some
oversteer (throttle-on, throttle-off or trail- braking).

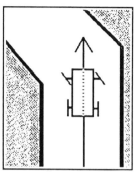

11 Understeer

The solution when you are <u>in the middle of understeer</u> is to correct the slip
angle of the front tires and get some weight on the front of the car.
Remember, the definition of understeer is that the slip angle at the front of the
car is more than at the rear. If the understeer is severe enough to <u>need</u>
correction, you are probably at a very high slip angle at the front of the car.

Sometimes steering corrections are all you need. Turn the steering wheel
somewhat (but not quite all the way) back toward center. This immediately
gets the slip angle back into a range where the tires can be effective. You will
immediately begin turning
more effectively. This step
is completely counter-
intuitive. You want to go

> *To correct understeer, lift the throttle and point the front tires more forward*

left, the car isn't going left, and now you are going to turn the wheel more to
the right. You have to experience it a few times before you will believe it.
The first few times you will have to <u>force</u> yourself to do it.

If you are pushing, you are forcing the front tires to slide sideways. If the
pushing is severe, the tires will not be rotating as fast as the car is going. As
long as the tires aren't rotating, they will have a tough time regaining traction
and giving you any help. The effect, until you get rid of the understeer
condition or get the steering wheel all the way back to pointing the tires
straight ahead, is that the further you turn the wheel back to the right, the
more the car goes left. As you point the tires more toward the direction the
car is actually traveling (rather than where you really wish it were going), the
tires begin rotating, provide more grip on track, and can apply more cornering
force. Your car begins to turn the direction you wish.

If you don't have the time or space to correct the understeer by steering
corrections alone, you will also need to get some weight onto the front tires.
In any case you must move the steering wheel back to where you want it to be

when the front tires hook up. Remember that you have already turned the wheel too far. If you add weight to the front without correcting the steering, you risk a rather quick transition from understeer to spin-inducing oversteer.

There are two ways to get weight onto the front of the car. You can reduce the amount of throttle (partially or all the way, as you deem appropriate based on the severity of the understeer). The deceleration caused by lifting the throttle will transfer weight to the front tires. If the reduction in throttle is not enough, then you can apply a small amount of brakes, transferring even more weight to the front tires. Such braking should be very minimal and should not be started until the tires are rolling properly.

The extent to which your car wants to understeer and oversteer, under various conditions, can be adjusted by rather simple adjustments to the suspension, as we shall see in the chapters on preparing your car. In this section the goal was limited to showing how to cope with and successfully exploit whatever behavior your car is exhibiting.

D. Turns & Shifting

The morning is grey but dry. The cars are not yet running, and all around the course people are walking, looking, sketching and discussing. At a four-pylon slalom connecting two right-hand corners, three of the fastest drivers are having a lengthy discussion of what might be the best line. The fast way into the slalom is to drive to the left of the first pylon, but this will put the car in bad shape to negotiate the second turn, at the far end of the slalom. On the other hand, getting the car inside (to the right) the first pylon will require a substantial reduction of speed through the entry turn. During most of the morning drivers try both lines, seeing if they can convince themselves that one approach is better than the other.

In this chapter we apply the basic driving techniques discussed in the previous chapter to the process of individual turns. There are several different turns, both by their individual shapes and by the ways in which they are linked to each other. Chapter E will explain how to apply the knowledge gained here to taking your best shot at an entire course.

Part 1: Turns & Lines

1. The Line (Where to Drive): First, use the entire width of the course. There is no centerline on the track, so you can use it all. Driving fast will involve using the edges of the course, first one side, then the other. As a general rule, you should NEVER DRIVE

> **Use the entire width of the course**

DOWN THE MIDDLE OF THE COURSE. You should be on one edge or the other, or be moving over to one edge or the other. The exceptions to this rule are where turns are linked so tightly that you can't finish one properly before you have to enter the next.

The 'line' down a straightaway is fairly unimportant except to connect the turn you just completed and the one you are going into next. The rest of this section will be devoted to the line through turns. While reading this, remember that you should always be thinking at least one turn ahead.

2. The Basic Turn: You are trying to <u>minimize</u> the sharpness of the turn and make it as smooth as possible. You want the biggest arc because your car can move faster if it isn't turning very much. If you stay along the inside of the course, from entry to exit, the turn would be very sharp. If you stay along the outside, life will be better, but not much. By starting from the outside, touching the inside during the middle of the turn, and then moving back to the outside, you have made the turn as gentle and straight as possible. Since you don't have to turn as sharply, you can go faster. We are trying to straighten out the turn as much as possible.

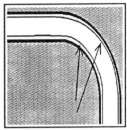

12 Wrong Lines

The <u>dictionary</u> defines 'apex' as 'the tip or point'. In competitive driving we care about the specific 'point' where you touch the inside of the turn. This is called the apex or the 'clipping point'. For any turn we can draw a smooth curve that will touch the outside of the course at the entry and exit of the turn, and touch the inside of the turn at some point. The largest-radius curve that will do this will touch the middle at the geometric apex. This would be your perfect line if you were going around the turn at a constant speed and had no particular preference about getting into the turn at high speed or getting <u>out</u> of the turn at high speed.

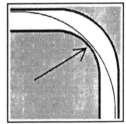

13 Geometric Apex

3. The Late-Apex Turn: The line through a turn that is most often used is <u>not</u> a geometric apex. Both in autocross and time trials, a turn that uses an apex point <u>later</u> than the geometric apex is often the best approach. There are several reasons for this. Not all reasons apply to every car in every turn, and not all apexes should be late. We will return to the topic of <u>exactly</u> where to place the apex in the next chapter. For now, what is needed is an explanation some of the reasons the late apex is a good line, and how to drive it.

3a. Why You Use a Late-Apex Line?: The first reason a late apex is often used is that you will often want to exit the turn at as high a speed as possible so the time you spend on the straightaway after the turn can be spent at the highest possible speed. It's not just that you want to be going fast at the end of the straight; rather, if you come out of the turn faster, you will cover every foot of the straightaway at a higher speed. When you exit slowly from a turn, you pay for it on every foot of track until the next time you have to hit the brakes. The longer the straightaway the more important it is that you exit the turn with the greatest speed possible. This can be more important in some corners than others, depending on what comes before and what lies after the particular turn in question, but, if in doubt, we normally want to come out of the turn as fast as possible. This is a sufficient reason for most late apexes, but there are sometimes other reasons as well.

The second reason for a late-apex line is to counteract oversteer. Cars that tend to oversteer, or, rather, a car proceeding through a turn in which that car will tend to oversteer, will normally corner better with plenty of throttle. The reason is that the acceleration transfers weight to the rear tires. Increasing the weight at the rear without increasing the mass at the rear will allow

> *If you come out of the turn faster you will cover EVERY FOOT of the following straight at a higher speed*

the tires to get a better grip, decreasing any natural oversteer tendency. Additionally, the weight transfer pushes the back of the car down, lowering the center of gravity at the rear of the car. This means that the car will tip less to the outside of the turn, leaving more weight on the inside rear tire. This is helpful, as, if the inside tire can help a bit more, you can go faster before the outside tire gets tired of the drill and lets go. The weight distribution of your car is important in all this. As a point of reference, rear-engined cars tend to oversteer, front engined cars tend to understeer. The tendency of any car will also vary with speed.

If you are cornering with the throttle on to counteract oversteer, the car will be accelerating, and the geometric apex will no longer work. The geometric apex presumes a constant speed through the turn. The line you want is one that will allow you to accelerate through the turn. Since the speed will be increasing, we know that you will be able to turn less sharply by the end of the turn, and will therefore have to be turning more sharply in the beginning. The line is no longer a constant-radius turn. Rather, it is somewhat sharp in the beginning, gradually straightening out as you come through the turn and gain speed. Positioning the most gentle such line we can devise into a turn, we find that the apex has moved further

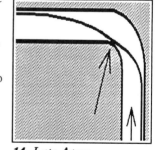

14 Late Apex

around the turn from the geometric apex. It is now a late-apex turn.

There is a third reason for using a late-apex line. It is the safest way to approach a high speed turn, and is therefore very important when

> *A late apex is the safest way to approach a high-speed turn*

learning to time trial. A late apex approach is much more forgiving of driver miscalculation. It forces the driver to brake earlier. If the driver misjudges the turn, there is more likelihood that the car will still be able to stay on the track. If you actually hit the late apex (as opposed to never getting to the inside edge of the course) it is difficult to be going fast enough to be forced off the course at the exit. A misjudged early-apex leaves very little room for error, and an early apex can be achieved at speeds high enough that there is no chance the car will stay on the course at the turn exit.

3b. How to Drive a Late-Apex Turn: The exact approach varies, depending on the car, the speed of the turn, and other factors; what follows is one approach. You come charging up to a turn. As much as needed before the turn, you get on the brakes hard, then get off them before you turn in. You do the braking in a straight line to accelerate through the turn.

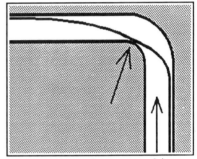

In this case you feed in at least some throttle JUST BEFORE you turn in. This is hard to learn, because you are entering the turn at a relatively high speed and your tendency is still to want to slow down. You will have to discipline yourself to do this, but the discipline will pay off. You have arranged it so you are well to the outside of the turn entry as you finish braking. Later than you would have thought, you turn the car in, and point it such that you will reach the inside of

15 Late-Apex (one example)

the turn somewhat later than the geometric apex. Sometime just before or at the selected apex you should have the throttle all the way down. This is the power point.

As you begin to feed in throttle, weight transfers to the back of the car. There are many reasons for a certain gentleness in feeding in throttle, and the beginning driver should avoid simply slamming down on the gas. First, cars with a very strong power-to-weight ratio on insufficiently sticky tires can often spin the rear wheels almost anytime the throttle is floored and the car is not pointed straight ahead. Second, moving from a braking condition to a throttle-on condition will transfer a great deal of weight from the front of the car to the back. The most successful transition (and the fastest turn) comes from smoothly bringing the rear suspension and tires to a fully-loaded condition without overshooting. You want to get the rear suspension reasonably well settled before asking it to do its maximum level of work. If you have done this well the cornering forces will move you and the car to the outside of the course at the exit of the turn, and you will just barely be able to avoid mowing down an entire row of innocent pylons. That is the late apex, and it is lots of fun.

If you turn in too late, you will not have as much room to turn the car. You will then either have to come into the turn slower than you might have been able to, or you will be unable to keep the car on course. If you turn in too early, you will find the apex in the way. This will force you to veer to the outside. Now you will be heading too much to the outside of the course, and you will have to turn again to keep from going off course, wasting time. You will also probably have to reduce the throttle somewhat. If you must err in deciding where to brake, brake too early rather than too late.

> *If you must err, brake too EARLY rather than too late*

Remember that the car will not quite go exactly where you point it in hard cornering. Where you point the car will have to be adjusted for the reactions you expect from the car.

3c. <u>Apex & Exit Precision</u>: In the discussion of starting at the outside of a turn, moving in to a late apex, then letting the car drift to the outside of the turn on the apex, it is important that you understand the precision involved. The precision is this: INCHES. If you are 10 inches away from the apex pylon, you are about 7 inches too far away. You won't be able to drive this precisely at first, given everything else you are trying to achieve. Once you <u>can</u> gauge things this closely you will find it much easier to get the lap times you want.

> *10 inches away from the apex pylon is about 7 inches too far away*

When you execute a turn with precision, the speed will force the car to the outside of the course at the exit of the turn. At times, you will not always execute with such precision and you may be going more slowly than needed. In those cases the car will <u>not</u> be forced to the outside of the turn. You nevertheless <u>drive</u> the car to the outside of the turn, to the exit point. The tires will roll better when you aren't asking them to turn as much. So, by following the line to the outside, the tires resist less and allow you to turn your horsepower into speed. You have already added time to your score by taking the turn slower than you might have. You can get a little of this time back by not asking the tires to turn the car more than is needed to keep you on the course.

4. <u>Very Slow Turns</u>: The special aspect of driving slow turns is to be sure that you slow down enough that you do not encounter severe understeer. Charging into such turns with excess speed will force you to go very slow indeed to get the car back where you wanted it. In very slow turns it is not possible to gain a lot of time, but it <u>is</u> possible to <u>lose</u> a lot of time. Get the car turned, then go.

5. Linked Turns: When two turns (one to the left, and one to the right) are linked together, followed by a somewhat straighter section, the key is to exit the second turn with the greatest speed.
This means that you may need to take a very different line in the first turn so you can do a proper, throttle-on, late-apex turn in the second turn. If you try to take a normal late-apex in the first turn, you may find that you are not at the

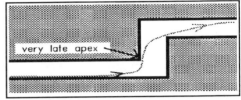

16 Linked Turns

right place, orientation or speed to do a good job on the second turn. In the example drawn, the main difference is that you would take an apex even later than normal on turn 1 to be in the right place for the entry to turn 2.

The second drawing shows what will happen if you do not make the first apex sufficiently late. At 'a' you can see that the apex is just slightly late. The car is then forced to exit the first turn to the outside, creating a very early apex for the second turn. Because of this, the exit from the second turn, 'b', finds the car pointed off the course. You will have to slow down a great

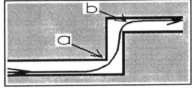

17 Wrong Way to Link Turns

deal to negotiate this turn, and your speed on the following section will be slow.

6. Slaloms: Autocross courses often feature a series of pylons set up in the middle of the course through which you must weave the car. This is not done at time trials. The series of pylons is called a slalom. When walking the course it is worth pacing off the distance between the pylons,

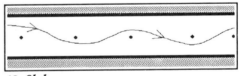

18 Slalom

to determine if they are all the same distance from each other, or if the distances vary. If they are all the same distance, then you may try to look for a pace that will weave you through them evenly. If the distances are not equal, then you will have to be aware of which parts can be taken faster than others. Sometimes a tipped cone will be used to show the path that the driver must follow through the slalom.

The basic approach in slaloms is similar to any other set of turns that are very tightly linked. The normal concepts of exit and entry may not apply. If your car is understeering, you will need to find a way to get the back end around. If your car wants to oversteer, you will need to apply some throttle as you turn around each pylon, and do any braking or throttle lifting that is needed in the little straight you get as you drive between the pylons.

During a slalom you will become especially conscious that
the car has a slightly delayed response to steering input,
and you will need to turn the wheels just a little before you
think you need the car to turn. This is actually always the
case when the car is operating near the limits of its
potential, but the effect is particularly noticeable when you
are running a slalom, because of the rapid back and forth
transitions.

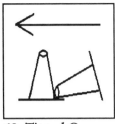

*19 Tipped Cone;
drive left*

The sensation of a slalom at moderate speed is quite
pleasant, a swaying back and forth. If in doubt, take the smooth approach; not a
Sunday drive, but don't get the car
unsettled. At the extreme limits of
car performance, there will be a lot
going on. On higher-speed
slaloms, you may need to be lifting

> *You will need to turn the steering
> wheel just a little bit <u>before</u> you
> think you need the car to turn*

the throttle or tapping brakes bit to get the car to do what you want it to do. All
this is tricky to coordinate and will require practice to become expert. You have
to learn to dance with the car.

7. Decreasing-Radius Turns: The approach to decreasing radius turns involves
simultaneously turning the car and slowing it through throttle lift or trail-
braking, both of which will induce oversteer. In
a turn that gets tighter and tighter, the basic
technique is to come in fairly fast ('hot'), turn in
to the beginning of the turn, and back off the
throttle enough to transfer weight to the front,
letting the back slide just a bit; add brakes if
needed. This will induce oversteer, tightening
your turn. The sliding of the rear tires will also
slow you down, making it possible to continue
to tighten the turn. Finally, when you have

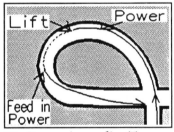

20 Decreasing-radius Turn

reached the <u>very late</u> apex, you can begin to feed in throttle, the back end will
begin to stick, and you can exit the turn under power.

Any attempt at a standard approach to early braking and throttle-on cornering
will either waste time and space in the beginning of the decreasing-radius turn, or
get you going so fast that you will not be able to complete the turn and stay on
course.
This is not an easy technique, and you should adjust your speed up (on successive
laps) in very small increments. Should you misjudge the speed which the car will
handle in this turn, you will very likely go off course.

8. Hairpins & Sweepers: Turns of more than 90° pose special challenges to the solo racer. Based on specific circumstances, you must decide which of several approaches to use.

> *In some cases, the best approach to a corner of more than 90° is to make two turns connected by a short straight*

8a. Sweepers: Late-Apex Approach: If the turn precedes a long straight section, it is very important that you leave the turn at the highest possible speed. In such cases you should use a late apex line. To do this you must stay wide in the entrance and travel further before turning than you would initially expect. The diagram shows a reasonable line, depending on the exact dimensions of the turn. This approach is somewhat counter-intuitive, and the rookie driver will almost always turn in too soon. You may need some opportunities to try different approaches until you agree that this really works. Of course, it is possible to go too wide (or, in racing talk, 'Stay out too long,') in some hairpin turns.

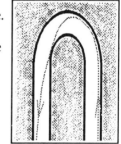
21 Hairpin Turn

8b. Sweepers: Hugging the Inside: If there isn't much of a straight after the sweeper you may be better off hugging the inside of the turn. This is particularly true if the turn is fast enough that you don't have to deal with any idiosyncracies that your car might have at very low speeds. The point of this approach is that you do not travel as far as if you took the late apex line. You may not be going quite as fast at the exit of the turn as a driver who took a late-apex line, but you will get to the apex quicker, since you traveled less distance.

22 Making Little Straights

8c. Sweepers: Making Little Straights: A third approach to a turn of more than 90°, is to try to make two or more turns out of it, with little straightaways between them. You can use the straightaways to get back on the throttle for a brief moment, and pick up a little bit of time. You will be faster in the little straights, and the scrubbing action of the tires will help you slow down and turn where you <u>are</u> turning. This approach is often the best one when the course is wide and the turn can be taken at a speed such that the car will handle relatively neutrally under power. A light car that turns easily will often respond especially well to this approach.

8d. Sweepers: Throttle Steering: The final approach that can be defined for this type of turn is a steady use of power-induced oversteer; the basic flat-track

approach. This takes some practice to master. It
can be a lot of fun, but there are some serious
disadvantages. First, it will tend to guide you into a
very even radius, usually not the fastest way into or
out of a turn. Second, and more importantly, in
most cars, you cannot fully use the throttle (as in
<u>push</u> <u>it</u> <u>all</u> <u>the</u> <u>way</u> <u>down</u>!) while using induced
oversteer. If your car is heavy, and reluctant to turn
quickly, but happy to corner once it gets set into a
turn, this approach will be a good bet for some turns.

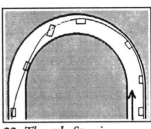

23 *Throttle Steering*

Two final thoughts about dealing with specific turns. First, and in all cases, make
sure you hit your apexes! Second, remember that the
ideal approach to any turn must consider the course
before and after the turn, as well as the capabilities of
the car. The next chapter will cover how to do that.

> *Hit your Apexes!*

Part 2: Shifting

9. Shifting: Some autocross courses have turns so tight that you must shift to
first gear to negotiate them and to accelerate out of them. Others have straight
sections long enough that you must use third gear. On a time trial course you
may be shifting ten or fifteen times a lap.

Shifting up to a higher gear is fairly straightforward. Just wait until the car is at
red-line or on the rev-limiter and be pretty quick about making the gear change.
Don't shift up if you need the higher gear for a very short time. You will waste
more time with the shifting than you will gain by the slight increase in speed for
a few yards of track. Rather, just hold the engine at or below red-line, then apply
your brakes before entering the next turn.

10. Downshifting: Downshifting properly is more difficult than upshifting for
two reasons: first, it usually happens while braking, so you have to coordinate it
with the braking; second, you need to rev the engine up so the car does not
become unsettled by a sudden change in engine speed.

The time for the downshift
is while braking before a
turn. You will be braking,
of course, since there would

> *The engine must be revved up to
> match the speed it will be going in the
> new gear*

be no reason to downshift if you weren't slowing down. You will want to come out of the turn in the lower gear, ready for brisk acceleration. Since you may be accelerating as early as the entry to the turn, you have to get into the lower gear before you enter the turn. You can do this while braking. Since you are braking enough to need a lower gear, you will likely be on the brakes long enough to complete the entire shifting process during braking.

The engine must be revved up so, when you let out the clutch, the rear tires won't have to do the work of getting the engine up to the speed that matches how fast the wheels are turning. The tires already have their hands (feet?) full, trying to cope with the aggressive braking you are doing and you don't want to make them undertake the extra work of revving up the engine.

But WAIT! It's not just the tires that are busy. YOU also have your hands and feet full, since the left hand is steering, the right hand is shifting, the right foot is working the brake and the left foot is pushing in the clutch. How are you going to get that throttle tapped for an instant to get the engine revs up? Read on.

11. Heel and Toe: This is the method of downshifting in which the left foot depresses the clutch and the right foot operates both the brake and the throttle. The throttle must be depressed to get the engine speed up to match the revs required at the current car speed in the newly-selected gear. If the transmission (synchromesh) is a little tired (or if the driver is trying to be especially nice to the transmission), then heel and toe will be used with double clutching to make the shift.

By classic definition, heel and toe refers to the process of using the front of the right foot to depress the brake while swinging the heel around to stab at the throttle. Usually a quick tap on the throttle is all that is required. The actual approach is to use the ball of the right foot on the right side of the brake pedal and then rotate the foot over to the right, allowing the right edge of the right foot to depress the throttle briefly. The accompanying illustration is not entirely clear about this. The right foot is actually placed so the ball of the foot is on the brake pedal and the right side of the foot is over the throttle pedal, but not yet touching the throttle. Then, when you need to blip the throttle, a rotation (or rolling over) of the foot will blip the throttle while allowing you to maintain pressure on the brake pedal. The foot doesn't move from side to side. The right side of the foot moves up and down as needed.

Some people attach a block of wood to the throttle pedal to help with heel-toe braking. It brings the surface of the throttle more nearly even with the surface of the brake pedal when the brake pedal is being used.

The process <u>without</u> double-clutching:

    depress brake pedal with right foot
    depress clutch pedal with left foot
    move shift lever to new gear,
    at the same time, quickly stab at
       the throttle with outside edge
       of your right foot
    once gearbox is in the new gear,
       release clutch
    release brakes

The process <u>with</u> double clutching:

    depress brake pedal with right foot
    depress clutch pedal with left foot
    move shift lever to neutral
    release clutch pedal
    quick stab at throttle with the
       outside edge of your right foot
    depress clutch pedal with left foot
    move shift lever to new gear
    release clutch
    release brakes

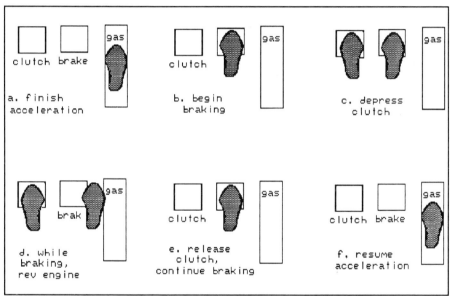

24 *Footwork for Heel & Toe*

It takes practice to be able to continue to apply the brakes evenly and firmly while blipping the throttle. You can do your initial practice in the driveway, parking brake on, car in neutral, engine running. You can also practice this on the street under moderate to heavy braking, but be <u>sure</u> to check your mirror before practicing severe braking or you may end up with someone's favorite family station wagon stuffed up your tailpipe.

12. <u>Timing the downshift</u>: If you are on the brakes for very much longer than it takes you to downshift, then you have to make a choice between downshifting when you <u>begin</u> braking, or downshifting at the end of braking.

You should work towards shifting at the last possible moment. Last-moment downshifting is easier on the car, may require less heel-toe, and is less likely to lead to an abrupt spin. It <u>does</u> take coordination, as you must time the beginning of your shifting activities so they complete just as your braking is complete and you are beginning to

> *Downshift as late as you can*

depress the throttle. You must also be dealing with the shifting when you would probably rather be paying absolute attention to setting up the car for the turn and getting the most out of your brakes. On the other hand, you have to be able to coordinate this properly anyway; this is exactly what you have to do when the braking time is just barely enough to complete a downshift.

Some people fall into a habit of shifting very early in the braking sequence. This gets the shift out of the way so you can concentrate on your braking and on getting set up just right for the entrance to the turn. However, downshifting at the higher speed is more difficult and somewhat harder on the car as the engine must be revved higher and the synchros will likely have to cope with a bigger mismatch. Further, if you downshift early in the braking and let out the clutch, you will add a lot of rear wheel resistance to the heavy braking you are already doing. This will tend to upset the equilibrium of the car, get the back end sliding around a bit and, if you are not braking in an absolutely straight line, may lead to a very quick spin. If you downshift early and <u>don't</u> let the clutch out, the engine revs will decrease while you brake. This defeats part of the purpose of heel-toe, as the rear tires will have to get the engine spinning once you <u>do</u> let out the clutch. You could blip the throttle <u>again</u>, but that is extra work and is getting pretty close to silliness.

A reasonable student approach is to work your way up to down-shifting at the last possible moment by trying to shift a little later during braking each time.

E. Optimizing Your Approach to the Complete Course

The car is pulling strongly up the back side of Laguna Seca. The engine temperature is fine, oil pressure where it belongs and the brakes haven't begun to fade. Before the crest, traveling on the left side of the track, he points the car to the apex of the slight dogleg to the right. On this line he can drive straight over the top of the hill and won't have to turn while the car is light. Just before the crest he taps the brakes slightly. He hates to do it, but it just isn't possible to do all the braking on the other side of the crest. As the car gets light on the crest he is off the brakes, but applies them firmly as the car begins to settle and the tires can get a grip. Under the hard braking the back of the car wants to wiggle, but doesn't, quite. Before he has completely released the brakes he begins the sharp left-hand turn, number 8. The tail of the car begins to move around to the outside. Just as it starts its move he begins to feed in throttle. The back end regains traction with the car having made about 60° of turn. He is already through 8 and heading for 8A. Rapidly, he feeds in the throttle and points the car to run over the middle of the berm slope on the inside of the sharp, downhill, right turn. As the car moves toward the turn exit and flatter terrain, it is drifting, pointed down the track but continuing to move to the side. As it begins to settle down at the exit, with about a foot of track width left, he turns the wheel to the right to get to the entry of turn 9, an off-camber left-hand turn, and can feel the tires operating at a slight slip angle. He checks the tach and finds the rpm 100 higher than the previous lap. "Lordy," he thinks, "I love how this car dances."

The chapter covers how to analyze a course and determine how to deal with each turn in it, then drive it optimally, making corrections as needed. The issues related to high-speed handling are normally relevant only to time trialing, but it is difficult to treat them as a completely separate discussion.

By the time you wish to <u>apply</u> the principles in this chapter you should be comfortable with basic car control. You should be able to be aggressive with the throttle and brakes, have good hand control on the steering wheel, be using the full width of the track, know what an apex is, and be comfortable with sliding and with throttle steering. If you drive where you need to shift the car you should be able to heel and toe downshift.

You should understand the terms entry, apex and exit. You should also be familiar with the basic types of turns, and be able to imagine and drive a competent line through linked turns, a slalom and decreasing radius and hairpin turns. If you think that sounds like you already have a lot of expertise, you are absolutely right. What else could you need to know about driving?

While all these skills are critical, they do not determine how to analyze a turn or a course. You need to determine and execute an optimal overall line and driving approach for the car being driven. Putting together a near-perfect lap is <u>the</u> goal in solo racing. The solo racer has no need for roadracing skills such as passing other cars. On the other hand, such skills also cannot be used to help compensate for less than optimal driving. The only help for the solo racer who has properly prepared the car is to find the fastest approach for the car, the way it is today, on the course, the way the course is today.

1. <u>Key Factors</u>: Before considering the course and deciding how best to attack it, we need to examine some basic issues related to car control and responsiveness. Let us imagine two different cars approaching a turn that is basically a 90° turn to the left and see what we can learn. For purposes of argument we will imagine that neither car has had extensive suspension modifications. Such modifications might make them more even to each other in certain instances, but would not change the basic differences between the cars.

In case one we have a very powerful car with a front engine, say a big-block, mid-sixties Corvette. Let us further imagine that it is running in a class that restricts it to tires of only moderate size. Because of the weight distribution, the car will <u>tend</u> to understeer at even moderate speed. In our example, this turn <u>is</u> slow. Further, since the car has easily enough

> *There is no <u>single</u> correct line*

power to spin the rear wheels coming out of the turn, the driver will be able to induce throttle-on oversteer at will. Our driver will approach the turn, apply the brakes, and probably trail-brake into the turn to help get the car turned. Unless there is room to use throttle-induced oversteer coming out of the turn, the driver is likely to wait until the car is pretty much through the turn before applying much throttle. Power applied before that point will tend to shift weight to the rear of the car, increasing understeer and interfering with turning. The driver will also probably have to wait until the car is almost completely straight before applying <u>full</u> throttle, lest the rear tires break loose and spin the car.

Consider now a different case. The turn looks the same <u>on paper</u>, but, in real life, is much wider and can be taken at a much higher speed. The car is a rear-engined car with a much lower power-to-weight ratio than the Corvette, say an early seventies Porsche 911T. It, too, is running on tires of moderate grip. Because the car has more weight in the rear than the front, it has a natural tendency to oversteer. Since the turn is being taken at high speed, this tendency is strongly increased. The motor isn't powerful enough to spin the rear tires, even at low speeds, and certainly not in the middle of a moderate to high speed turn. Since oversteer will be the key issue in this turn, the driver is likely to do all the braking before the turn. Trail-braking will <u>not</u> be used. Further, in an effort to decrease oversteer, the driver will likely have the throttle completely to the floor before even beginning the turn. The throttle will be kept to the floor throughout the turn.

So, the turn looks the same on paper, but the approaches used by these two drivers are just as different as they can be. The line used, when the brakes are applied, when the throttle is applied and by how much, all are different. If we could take the drivers from these two cars, and watch exactly how they drive the turns, and listen to them describe the techniques they are using, you would almost believe that they are talking about two entirely different sports. Both may be doing all the right things for the car and turn they are driving.

> *You must consider:*
> - *available traction*
> - *available power*
> - *speed of the turn*
> - *your car's handling*
> - *your preferences*

What we learn from this is there is not a single line we can draw on paper and claim that it is the 'right' line. Actually, the examples are overdrawn. The cars are so different that, for most moderate-speed turns, the cars will need to be driven somewhat differently, even when driven through the exact same turn.

When determining how you are going to approach a course or a turn, you must understand the factors that determine the proper approach and apply them to each course and turn you drive. The factors are highly inter-related, and you must take them all into account. Even if you have lots of engine power on tap, what you do with it will depend on existing traction and the handling characteristics of your car. So what are these factors that you must consider before you determine how you take any turn in your car? They are available traction, available engine power, the speed of the turn, the handling characteristics of your car and your own preferences.

1a. Available Traction: You must examine the course and have a reasonable sense of the available traction at all points on the course. The basic composition of the road surface is important (concrete doesn't usually provide as much traction as asphalt, for example). If the track is bumpy, you will have less effective grip with your tires.

Any water on the track will be very important, particularly if you are running race tires, which are much worse in wet conditions than just about any other tire. Oil can also be a serious problem. Cars sometimes break some part of their oil system and deposit oil on the track. This is cleaned up as well as possible, of course, but the residual

| *Know the traction at all points on the course* |

can cause slipperiness. With water and oil, you have to imagine the area of reduced traction to be where the liquid is, and then further on down the track until your tires clean themselves off, which they will gradually do. You will have to feel how long it takes for the tires to recover, and allow yourself some margin until you are sure they are back to normal.

Rainy racing (just autocross; most clubs will not run time trials in the rain) is a lot of fun, but will force you to make major changes in your approach. Power oversteer will be available to almost all cars at all points on the course. You may also find yourself beating cars you could never catch on a dry track, and losing to cars that usually aren't within 3 seconds of your times.

Gravel, sometimes called marbles, can play a big role in traction and line selection. If you are one of the first 20 or so cars to run at an autocross, you will find that the track has not been quite cleaned off yet. Even if people with brooms or blowers have tried to get the track clean, it takes a few cars to get the track right. Even then, there will be marbles where people have not been driving. The same is true on a road track. If you are off a reasonable line, the traction may be quite poor indeed. You must keep the gravel in mind if you have a very different idea than the other drivers at the event of what the proper line should be. I have more than once had to submit to the will of the majority and drive their line, because the line I wanted to use had too much gravel left on it.

Time of day affects the track at a one-day autocross. Even after the gravel is pretty much moved out of the way, the course usually gets

| *The course gets faster during the day* |

faster and faster during the day, as small amounts of rubber are laid down at key points. The rubber on the surface increases traction.

The brand, size, model and condition of your tires will also affect traction. Normally, you will want to have the best tires possible on the car at important races. There will be times when you end up running on less than optimum rubber, and you need to allow for the reduced traction in planning turn speeds and braking points.

Temperature will affect traction. Exactly what the effect is will depend on the type and brand of tires you are running. For street tires, it seems that a warmer temperature affords better traction. If you are time trialing at a track where you already know what sorts of times to expect, you may occasionally find that you simply can't go as fast this weekend. If the traction is less than the last time you were here, you <u>will</u> turn slower times. So, if the temperature is much different from normal, you need to be ready to adjust your expectations about your lap times. Don't try to go faster than feels reasonable just because your times are not up to your expectations!

The contour of the course will also affect available traction. Obviously, if the turn is banked, you will be able to go faster. Conversely, if the turn is off-camber (sloped to the outside), you will take the turn more slowly. There is less traction heading downhill and more traction

> *A crest or bump may dramatically reduce your traction*

heading uphill. A bump or crest will tend to unweight the car, reducing traction dramatically. On the other hand, the bottom of a dip, or the point at which a downhill ends will afford much greater traction. If you are driving a course that moves up and down, you will find some turns at the bottom of a hill that you don't think you can take any faster, until you experience how much extra traction you get from the bottom of the dip. Understanding such points on the track as these can be critical to staying out of trouble and to decreasing lap times.

There are two possible responses to severely reduced traction. If it is localized, like a puddle of water, or a gravely spot, you might be able to design a line that drives you around it. If you cannot drive around it, you need to reduce cornering speeds, increase braking distances and reduce the amount of throttle you apply when the car is still turning. You also need to plan to adjust to increased traction. At an autocross, if you ran effectively early in the day, when the course wasn't yet quite cleaned off, your next try needs to count on having somewhat more traction available. So you drive somewhat more aggressively. If you don't make this adjustment, your times will suffer.

1b. Available Engine Power: Having ample engine power available means that you are more able to induce throttle-on oversteer at will. If you already have enough oversteer this means that you must be judicious in your use of the throttle. When you want the oversteer to serve a particular function, or want to counteract understeer, you may be able to induce it by applying more throttle than you need for acceleration.

Keep in mind that using throttle-induced oversteer <u>can</u> translate a lot more energy into tearing up tires than into propelling your

> *Throttle-induced oversteer can tear up your tires <u>and</u> slow you down*

car forward. Outside of counteracting understeer, inducing oversteer is only occasionally the fastest way through a turn. You are simply not operating at the optimal slip angle for the tire. (One exception is dirt-track racing, where the ideal approach is to use massive oversteer to point the entire car toward the direction you want to turn, then apply lots of power.)

When using the available engine power to induce oversteer or simply to overpower the rear tires when accelerating in a straight line, keep in mind that you get optimal tire traction when the tire is slipping just a little bit against the course surface. Outside of the realm of drag race starts, spinning the rear tires rapidly will be slower than spinning them just a very little bit.

Available engine power will also affect your line selection in the moderate-speed turns. If you have a great deal of power compared to the weight of your car (and if you are also not battling severe natural understeer), you may be able to accelerate quite a bit through the turn. To do this effectively you must design for yourself a fairly late apex, since your increasing speed requires a larger diameter radius after the apex.

1c. How Fast is the Turn?: There is an approximate maximum speed at which any given car will negotiate any given turn. This speed is a function of the traction available to the tires, the handling characteristics of the car, and the diameter of the arc one could draw of the car's

> *Higher-speed turns will have apexes that are more neutral, less late*

approximate line through the turn. The approximate speed of the turn should influence how you design your line.

The higher the speed of the turn, the less likely it is that you will need to induce oversteer by throttle lift or aggressive trail-braking, and the more likely it is that you will want to keep enough throttle applied to keep weight transferred to the back of the car. On the slower turns, of course, the reverse is true. On slow turns you may be looking for ways to counteract understeer.

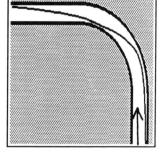

25 *Good Low-Speed Late Apex*

The higher speed turns will have apexes that are more neutral, and less late. The reason for this is simple. On the faster turns your speed at the entry to the turn and the exit of the turn will be more nearly equal, therefore the arc you want to drive is more nearly the same for the first and second halves of the turn. The more the arcs are, in fact, the same, the more neutral the apex will be. The two drawings may help clarify this. Check them carefully.

Experienced autocrossers often have trouble with this point when they begin time trialing, and, therefore, working with higher-speed turns. In autocross, drivers normally have to learn to stay wide until later than they think appropriate in order to achieve a proper late apex. The higher-speed turns still have late apexes, but they work differently and look different from inside the car. As soon as you have completed your braking and begun (at the correct point on the track!) turning in, you need to move the car towards the apex pretty rapidly. Then, during the middle part of the turn, you hold the car in, and it feels like you are just creeping toward the apex, inch by inch. After you pass the apex point the speed and acceleration of the car will force you to the outside of the turn, just like autocross and just like you had planned. If you find that the first part of the turn seems very easy for you, you may not be moving the car into the apex rapidly enough.

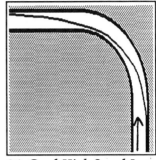

26 *Good High-Speed Late Apex*

1d. Handling Characteristics of the Car: The basic handling characteristics of the car have a dramatic effect on the techniques and line selection used by a driver. If the car tends to oversteer, you design lines that do not involve trail-braking or throttle lift in high-speed turns and you will need to plan to enter turns with more throttle on. On the other hand, if your car tends to understeer except at very high speed you will need to use more trail-braking and you may need throttle lift, throttle-induced oversteer or even left-foot braking in the slower turns.

Over the long haul, you <u>may</u> want to make suspension modifications to your car to induce more neutral handling. On the other hand, you may be happy running in your current class, and may have to limit yourself to the allowed suspension adjustments.

While you are learning these techniques of handling a car at the limits of its potential, watch your own learning process and be aware of the extent to which the handling characteristics of your current car are encouraging you to drive in certain ways, to approach turns with certain styles.

> *Watch your own learning process: be aware of the directions you are being pushed by the way your car handles*

When you see two very good drivers approaching a course with similar machinery but with noticeable style differences, you might be correct in hunching that these drivers learned their skills in cars that had very different handling characteristics.

You can learn more about all this by intentionally setting your suspension to one end of the spectrum or the other, or by driving a variety of cars. At some point in your learning this is almost essential. Once you have experience driving a range of cars, you will have a better sense of what yours does well and what could be improved.

1e. Driver Preference: Some drivers prefer to have the car sliding very little. Others prefer more sliding. Both of these drivers may be operating near the optimum slip angle of the tires. What one driver considers a good approach may seem overly mild or overly aggressive to another driver. You will often hear drivers, when discussing a particular turn, use the

> *What one expert driver considers to be a good approach may look overly mild or overly aggressive to another expert driver*

phrase, "What I like to do in that turn . . .", [emphasis added]. This is an honest and correct statement. It is what they like.

When designing your line, take into account the way you like to drive the car. This should not be the dominant factor in your design, as it is easy to get a bit carried away. People may say, "Do whatever you like," or "Do whatever works for you," avoiding any further discussion of what really does work. 'Whatever you like' may not be fine, and may not be the fastest way around the track. You need to find

> *Find a healthy balance between trusting your instincts and looking for a better approach*

a healthy balance between trusting your instincts and preferences, and being ever on the lookout for better ways to drive.

2. Full-course Line Selection: To analyze a complete course, start by looking for the longest straights. A straight does not have to be completely straight. Rather, it is a section of the course where, using optimal driving techniques, you will not need to lift your foot from the throttle or apply the brakes. During these sections you will be under constant acceleration.

2a. Late-Apex Turns: The most important turns are the ones preceding the longest straights. Alan Johnson (see Bibliography) calls these turns Type I Turns. For these turns you will want to design a line that allows you to get the throttle all the way to the floor as early as possible, even if you have to give up a little speed

> *The most important turns precede the longest straights*

getting into the turn. The line through this turn will normally be a late apex. However, the proper evaluation of the turn is simply to find the earliest point where you can place the car in the proper orientation so you can get the throttle <u>completely</u> <u>down</u> without inducing a lot of oversteer or rear-wheel spin. The extra speed you gain from exiting this turn faster will pay off immensely during the entire straight, since you will be traveling every foot of the straight faster than if you had used an inferior line in the turn just before the straight.

You may sometimes have a difficult time believing that you are doing the right thing, trying for these late apexes in the slow turns. In tight autocross courses, you may find that you have to slow down a tremendous amount to get the car pointed in the correct direction and ready to accept maximum acceleration. When you can, try

> *Sometimes you have to go slow in order to go fast*

it both ways. The slower entrance but faster exit from a turn in front of an important straight is the <u>only</u> reasonable approach. It is said that, sometimes, you have to go slow to go fast. These turns are what that adage is about.

<u>2b. Early-Apex Turns</u>: The second-most important turns are the ones at the END of a straight section. Johnson calls these Type II Turns. If these turns don't

> *Do not late-apex every turn you find*

also begin a significant straight, you should use an early apex. This is just about the only time an early apex should be used in solo racing. [In roadracing the inside entry to the turn can be a nice place to pass. And, if you are on that line, the person behind you can't use it to pass you. Of course, such considerations are not relevant to autocross or time trialing.]

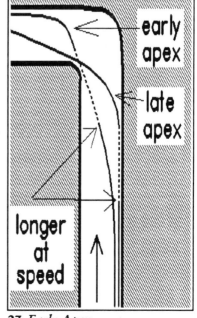

You don't use the early apex for any reasons associated with the turn itself. You will come out of the turn more slowly than if you had used a late apex. However, the early-apex line allows you to stay on the throttle longer, holding all that speed that you have built up on the preceding straight, covering the track distance at a high rate. Once you have the speed, you want to hold on to it as long as you can. So, at the end of a straight, you should brake as late as possible. Be very careful of gravel (marbles) at the turning point (after the apex) when trying an early apex. If no one else is using the line, you may well be off into an area of very poor

27 Early Apex

traction. This is unlikely to get you a fast time, and may be dangerous.

How does an early apex help you delay braking? By turning the car slightly at the entry point, you will find there is more track in front of you (than if you hadn't turned), so you can brake later. The illustration shows how much longer you can travel at the higher speed. The dotted lines are the sections used for braking.

If the straight before the turn is long enough and the straight after the turn is relatively short, the early apex is your best bet. You already have time in the bank, as it were, since you have delayed braking and are ahead of where you would have been, had you put the brakes on early and prepared for a late apex. Keep in mind, you <u>will</u> exit the turn more slowly, so don't use an early apex before a straight of any serious length, no matter how long the preceding straight was. You will lose more than you gain.

2c. <u>Other Turns and Considerations</u>: What about the rest of the turns, which are at neither end of a significant straight and are not any of the special turns covered in the previous chapter? In general you will be looking for a late apex, but you should consider <u>all</u> the factors as you plan your approach.

When turns get very slow, you should worry less about late apexes and more about just finding a smooth line through the tight stuff. I have seen drivers traveling at very slow speeds going way out of their way to set up for a late apex in situations where there was no

> *When things get very slow and tight, do not try for super-late apexes*

chance of being able to apply any serious amount of throttle because there were three more tight turns waiting. The point to watch for, when you come out of a slow section, is the point at which you can seriously begin to feed in throttle. The sooner you can get on the throttle, the better off you will be.

You will find that it is often impossible to design a line that is good for each turn when there are many turns linked together. The proper exit from one turn makes it impossible to have a proper entry for the next. In these cases be sure you don't compromise on the last turn before the straight. Besides that, be steady. You can lose a lot more time going too slowly in one turn than you will probably make up by going a bit faster through the next one, so be suspicious of a line that gets you too far below a reasonable speed.

Be sure that your approach has an overall smoothness to it. If you focus too much on just the individual turns and how you want to optimize them, you may find yourself jerking the car around too much as you finish one

> *Find a <u>smooth</u> line*

turn and prepare for the next. When things are happening very quickly, it is better to emphasize smoothness than to force the car into classic entry, apex and exit points at each turn. Loading and unloading the tires and suspension very rapidly will prevent your car from doing its best. You paid for four good tires and you deserve to have their best efforts. You won't get their best efforts if you hurry them too much. If you must choose between smoothly loading the tires and suspension, or being in the ideal place, try to err on the side of smoothness.

Try to plan a tolerant line when planning your overall approach. A tolerant line is one which allows you to correct minor miscalculations and still turn in a reasonable lap time. An approach that leaves no room for error will fail when you make a small error. In time trials, a very early apex may be an OK approach if the outside of the turn is a nice flat dirt surface that goes on and on, with no solid objects to hit. An early apex in situations where the outside of the turn is a brick wall is an entirely different proposition, and should be taken much more carefully and more slowly.

3. What is in your Design? In the discussion of the process of designing an approach to the entire course and each turn in it, keep in mind that the design is not something you do before you drive the course, think about during the first lap, then forget altogether. It is an evolving entity. If you have only walked the course, you may have only

> *A design is not put away after you drive the course; rather, it is continually refined*

hunches about how some of this will work out and how your car will respond. After a few laps, you should be able to shut your eyes and drive the course, both the way you just did it and the way you want to do it. The design you are driving should evolve each time you drive the course, and can become more precise about exactly what is working and what is not. Where things don't work as you expected, you change your approach.

3a. The Line: The first part of the design, of course, is the basic line you plan to follow around the course. This is not just the location at which you want to place the car, but also the direction you expect it to be pointed. That is, you should have a reasonable idea how much slip angle you will be using, and whether you expect to be contending with understeer or oversteer.

3b. Throttle Control: Next, you need to know what you will be doing with the throttle for the entire course. This means more than just knowing the power point of each turn (the place where you begin to feed in throttle), though that is important, of course. You also need to be conscious of those sections where you will want to use throttle, but not be able to use it all.

3c. <u>Brake Control</u>: You need to have clear ideas about brake points, including any places where you will be using less than full braking, or be braking while turning. The best drivers use landmarks as braking reference points. By doing this they are able to make small adjustments in the brake points, based on whether they are ending up in the turn at too high or too low a speed. Pay close attention to sections where you are planning to be braking and turning at the same point, hunching carefully where on the friction circle you will be operating.

3d. <u>Shifting</u>: You should have a good notion of whether or not you will be shifting, and, if so, where. The only true difficulty around shift points comes when you run out of available engine revs just a little before you will have to be on the brakes. The better you can heel-and-toe

> *The better you heel & toe shift, the better you can use the track*

downshift, the shorter space you need to go ahead and shift up. However, no matter who you are or how you drive, there will be stretches before brake points where you aren't sure that it is worth the effort to shift up then back down. If the turn is fast, and you can use the higher gear through it and beyond, then it's an easy choice again; go ahead and shift.

There are two important considerations about shifting up then down. First, acceleration is always important, and you may gain a substantial advantage shifting for a relatively short section of track, if you don't lose more time doing your downshift while braking. Second, if you decide not to shift, you may find that the slightly slower speed you bring to the turn allows you a different and more effective line. You might, for example, take a later apex line on a turn that you would otherwise early apex. In this way you will pick up a little of the time during and after the turn that you lost by not being able to shift up when the car wanted you to.

If you find that you need to shift in the middle of acceleration during a turn, you need to try to revise your approach. Such shifting will be very unsettling to your car, so

> *Avoid shifting in a turn*

you will not be able to corner at its limits. Better to find a point before you get to maximum cornering to do your shifting. Short-shifting (shifting up a car before it needs to be shifted) a car that has a broad torque range will not lose very much acceleration.

4. <u>Revising the Plan as You Drive</u>: In autocrossing you will normally rely on a coursewalk to design your approach to a course, since, in most cases, the course was built by a group of people that morning, and will never before have been seen by human eyes. Then, after each run, you need to review what happened to refine your design. Most people don't walk the full length of a roadracing track,

so time trialers normally just take it very easy during the first practice session, then begin to formulate their plan. If you have previous experience driving this track during some other weekend, then you should have a pretty good design in mind before you drive. After each practice session, you will need to review and revise. Track conditions change, car and tire capabilities change over time, and things don't always work out as expected. The final judge is always the stopwatch.

If you cannot get the power on where you wanted to, decide whether your original plan was incorrect, or you just need to go more slowly to get the car turned in time. If you were counting on induced oversteer to swing the back end around at some point, and are having a difficult time getting the car to rotate, decide whether the plan was correct, or whether the car would be happier (and faster!) doing something else.

> *The final judge is the clock*

If you can, get someone to time you through <u>sections</u> of the course while you try alternative approaches. Driving an entire course you will execute some turns well, others less well. It is not always possible to tell from the lap time whether the one thing you intended to do differently is helping or not.

By watching your tachometer at specific points in the course you may get an idea of whether a different approach is working. You have to check it at the same point on the track, of course, and you should have the road situation well enough in hand that you can afford to take your eyes off the road for a brief moment. Having rotated your tachometer (if possible) so redline is just a bit beyond vertical will probably help you, since you will be operating near redline at most times and can count on the needle being somewhere near the top.

> *Watch the tachometer*

5. <u>Optimal Driving, Realtime</u>: While you are driving, there are some specific considerations about how you handle the car. When you get down to trying to fine tune tenths of seconds off your time, small matters of style can become very important.

5a. <u>Watch the Apex</u>: As you pass an apex and see that you are on a reasonable path to the exit of the turn, immediately locate the apex of the next turn and focus your attention on it. This is important in all cases except where you are entering a long straight. By always driving in reference to the next apex, you will have an easier time setting up your next turn correctly. If you fail to do this, the turn will tend to take you by surprise, and you will find yourself in the wrong place or at the wrong speed for the turn.

> *Focus on the next apex*

5b. Be Early with Steering: The very first reaction from the car, when you turn the wheel, is that the outside suspension compresses as the weight shifts to the outside. As the suspension compresses, the tires are also compressing, and the side forces begin to force the shoulder of the tire to roll under a bit. Then the tires begin, ever so slightly, to slip to the side. This is always true, but nearly imperceptible at moderate speeds. Finally the car stabilizes in the turn. When you are driving near the limits, this delay in car response will be important, and you will need to learn to feed in steering input just a fraction of a second <u>before</u> you really want the car to begin turning. The effect is more noticeable at slow speeds.

5c. Loading the Tires and Suspension during Braking: If you jam on the brakes, you will 'surprise' the tires, and they will begin to lock up. On the other hand, if you apply them gently at first, then quickly increase the pressure, the tires and brakes will do a lot of work for you.

You also need to be conscious of suspension and tire loading when transitioning from braking to turning. Under hard braking you have the front suspension of the car fully loaded. If you lift off the brakes, then turn the wheel, the outside front corner of the car will rise, then have to compress again. Try to begin turning as you release the brakes, keeping the outside front corner constantly loaded. If your car is tautly suspended you will not see the corner bobbing around very much, but the smoothness in loading will help the suspension and tires work effectively.

5d. Initiating the Turn: If you begin your turn <u>very</u> gently, you will find that you are wasting time. This turn-initiation time is not under maximum braking, since you can't do maximum braking and turn at the same time. It is not yet under full acceleration. You haven't yet reached the

> *Bring the suspension and tires to full load without overshooting*

cornering limits of your car, so it is not time that is being used for maximum cornering. Such an approach is slower than if you spent the time doing something at the limit.

On the other hand, you do not want to jerk the car around. If you make very rapid movements with the steering wheel (or brakes or throttle, for that matter), you will rapidly and <u>excessively</u> load the suspension of the car and the tires, with bad effects. Remember that <u>every action</u> changes tire and suspension loading. Abrupt actions create abrupt changes in loading.

You will find the right compromise by feeling how your

> *Every action changes tire loading*

suspension responds. The actual speed with which you can initiate turning will depend on your particular suspension. The effect you want is to bring the suspension and tires to full load without overshooting. Many drivers have talked about striving to have 'slow hands', which is one way to attune yourself to driving within the limits of the suspension, letting it help you as much as it can. Jackie Stewart has an exercise in which the student tries to keep a ball in the middle of a large dish on the hood of the car while negotiating a course. Same thing. If you jerk the car to the side, the ball will fly out, but, if you load the suspension smoothly and firmly, the ball will stay in place. Try to remember the words of the famous and very successful (10 NCAA championships in 11 years) basketball coach for UCLA, John Wooden, who told his players, "Be quick, but don't hurry."

5e. Optimizing the Slip Angle: While driving, feel the tires operate and be conscious of the slip angles of the tires. Dramatic sliding is rarely the fast way. If you are fighting with plow (understeer) in the slow turns, induce oversteer through trail-

> ## *High slip angles slow the car down*

braking or throttle lift. If you have the tail hanging out in slow turns, get on the throttle earlier, or with less force.

As you go through a turn with proper slip angles, you will notice a subtle sensation of hanging the inside front tire over the apex point, as you pass it. The inside tire is light, weight having been transferred to the outside. The car is pointed a bit to the inside, due to the slip angle of the car.

5f. Hit the Apexes: You may enter a turn so fast, or be a little late in beginning to turn in, that you don't think you can get all the way to the inside to make a proper apex. You may think you have to settle for coming around the turn a little wide and miss touching the apex point. When this happens, keep the car smooth, but force the car in to the apex anyway! This is particularly important in time trials,

> ## *Hit the apex!*

where the consequences of leaving the track are usually unpleasant. Even if you are sure the car will not go to the apex, turn in and hit the apex! In general, if the car handles reasonably, and you hit the apex pointed even approximately forward, you have a very good chance of staying on the track. If you smoothly but quickly increase the slip angle (which is what will happen if you force the car in to the apex when it doesn't feel like it wants to go there), you will find that the car will scrub off speed due to the extra drag of the tires. This may get you through the turn. If you were going too fast, you won't get through the turn with any style points, and later you should think carefully about what got you to that point at that speed, but the scrubbing will definitely help. Remember, this is not a discussion of a general approach to time trial turns. Rather, it is a discussion of your proper response to a marginally out-of-control situation. This can get dicey at higher speeds. Many cars are not terribly stable under high slip angles at high speeds. If your car has vicious oversteering tendencies, you will have to be especially smooth as you point it in toward the apex.

5g. Leaving the Track in Style: On a road course, if you do find yourself unable to avoid heading off the course at speed, straighten the front wheel and relax the throttle to the point that the car is neither accelerating nor decelerating. If you are drifting the back of the car when leaving the pavement, the back will leave the pavement first, and will immediately lose most of its traction. The rear of the car will then begin to spin around to the front. Often the car will stabilize just after it completes a 180° turn and shoot backwards across the track to the inside of the turn. You may be able to avoid this if you are not drifting when you leave the track. You do this by straightening the front wheels. All this is not to frighten you; many people time trial for years and never get more than two wheels off into the dirt. However, if you should need it, it will be good if you have mentally practiced what you would do in such a situation.

5h. Handling Unexpected Loss of Traction: Unexpected, in this context, simply means you didn't expect the car to be sliding nearly this much. In autocross it normally means that you have erred on the side of exuberance as you entered a turn. In time trials it can mean that you have encountered some oil left on the track by a car traveling

> *When you are losing control of the car, keep the steering wheel and throttle very steady*

in front of you. If you are spinning, simply put in the clutch and apply the brakes. You will stop wherever you stop. There are no drivers who can recover from all spins, and there are few who can recover from most spins.

If you are still relatively under control, try to stay very steady with the steering wheel and throttle, and gently but quickly release the brakes if you are using them. The action you take will depend on where the car is headed and what the dangers are, but smoothness will be your greatest ally.

5i. Optimizing Inside Exits: While on course you will sometimes find that you have taken a turn more slowly than you might, and that you are not forced to an exit point all the way to the outside edge of the course. Most of the time you should drive out to the outside edge of the course anyway. Your tires will have less cornering to do, you will operate at lower slip angles, and your car will be able to accelerate better, salvaging a little bit of time from your mistakenly slow turn. However, if you are in the midst of a series of tightly linked turns, you may find that your inside exit makes it possible to take a more effective line in the next turn. When this happens, be sure to adjust your line to take advantage of the situation.

5j. Dealing with Brake Fade: Brake fade is almost never an issue at an autocross or during time trial timed runs, but can become an important issue during time trial practice sessions. Brakes will fade when they have absorbed all the heat they can and have insufficient ways to get rid of it. It takes much longer for brake fade to go away

> *Brakes become very important in time trials*

than it does for it to appear. Usually, your brakes will begin to be slightly less effective before they become dramatically less effective. If you haven't been paying enough attention to the brakes, the onset of fade can be extremely unnerving. The effect is that you push down hard on the brakes, and the car does not slow down very much. As it turns out, there are usually options available to the driver, and a little brake fade doesn't usually lead to bent sheet metal. Partial brakes, along with the scrubbing of the tires, as the driver turns in for the apex, will usually keep the car under control and on the track. On the other hand, brake fade can be unnerving, and deserves careful attention.

As you are driving, try to be aware of how much effort it takes to bring the car to full braking. If this effort seems to be increasing a bit, begin to use earlier braking points. If nothing changes dramatically, then everything may have been fine all along. However, if the brakes fade dramatically, you will be really glad that you were using an earlier braking point.

F. Beyond Autocross: Time Trials

She charges over the hill, brakes briefly, then turns the car to the left, looking for the proper apex at turn 6, The Carousel. It is Saturday morning of her fourth time trial ever, and only her second time at Sears Point. The suspension is working hard and the tires are complaining, but the car is nowhere near the limit. She is still learning, knows it, and is driving within her limits. Having come in a bit hot, she fails to nail the apex, and eases the throttle just a bit. Her pulse rate increases as the adrenalin hits her blood system almost immediately. She was already pretty tense once she got on the track, cars everywhere and so much to remember and try to do precisely. There is adequate room to stay on the track as she exits turn 6, and she heads up to turn 7, a hairpin, under full throttle. "Gee," she thinks, "I'm driving sloppy. I thought these first-practice-session jitters were behind me."

You may find, after you have been autocrossing for awhile, that the sport, while tremendous fun, is not completely satisfying. You spend long hours driving to events and a substantial amount of time at the events, mostly working and socializing. You do all this for a very few runs on the course. Granted, the runs are exciting, the people at the event are enjoyable to be with, the car is fun to drive, and you may have the pleasant company of a spouse or friend traveling to and from the events. Nevertheless, you find yourself wanting more track time. You are not alone in this. It is a feeling shared by many autocrossers. Fortunately, in many parts of the country, there is an option, more or less. That option is called time trials or SCCA Solo I. You could, of course, decide to go wheel-to-wheel racing, but you do not have to make that commitment to get lots of track time.

> *You find yourself wanting more track time*

Time trials are not 'beyond' autocross in <u>any</u> sense of skill required. To succeed at either sport, you need to be a very knowledgeable and precise driver. A good autocrosser must be able to learn a new course very rapidly, perhaps only getting three shots at a course before it is torn down, never to be seen in quite that form again. To be able to drive with fast precision during your second lap on a course is a difficult skill to master. Time trialers, on the other hand, often practice a course for 30 or 40 laps before running for time, and may return to the same course several times a year for a few years.

Time trials are 'beyond' autocross in terms of risk. Because of this, it is sometimes said that autocross is a test of skill, and time trials are a test of courage. This isn't exactly true. Time trials are a test of skill <u>and</u> courage. Because of the risk, it is my very strong belief that people should autocross before time trialing. A

> *Learn to autocross before attempting time trials*

reasonably diligent student should learn enough in 10 or 15 autocross events to be ready for time trialing, but twice that would be better. In autocross, the limits of the car (at more moderate speeds) can be learned within a great margin of safety. The driver will have translated the correct throttle, brake and steering corrections for various levels of drifting and sliding into automatic reactions. There is a lot going on when cars are time trialing, and much for the driver to do. The experience of autocross makes time trialing a car much safer.

Time trialing is also beyond autocross in cost. There are additional expenses for safety equipment, it is harder on the car, tires wear out very fast, and the entry fees are normally in the range of $100 and up for two days (compared to about $20 for two days of autocrossing). For that additional money you get to spend a lot more time driving. Cost per minute for autocrossing track time varies between roughly $2 and $4. Cost per minute for time trialing runs between $1 and $2, not a huge difference. However, <u>your</u> total time is also important, and you get about seven time as much track time per racing day going time trialing.

1. What is a Time Trial?: A time trial is an event in which cars run for best lap time on a road-racing track. Time trials are conducted by various car clubs. SCCA has an active program under the title of Solo I. Marque-oriented clubs, such as the Porsche Club of America, have programs in certain parts of the country. There are variations in how these various time trials are run, but much of what follows will be true for most time trials.

> *If I must go around in circles . . . at least let them be big ones*
>
> ©1983 Ashleigh Brilliant; Pot-Shot No.3051. Used by permission

A time trial is similar to an autocross in that you compete against other people by trying for the fastest time. However, this all takes place at a real roadracing track, at much higher speeds. It is a chance to take your car out onto the same road courses used by SCCA, CART, Winston Cup and other racing series. The tracks are normally 2 to 3 miles long, and will have roughly 8 to 14 turns. There is no traffic coming the other directions, and there are no gendarmes to take exception to your judgement about what is a reasonable allowance above the national speed law. This does NOT mean that there are not reasonable limits for driving, even under track conditions. You will be required to operate your vehicle so as not to endanger yourself or others. Time trials are not wheel-to-wheel races; you can expect that people will not be leaning on your fenders going through the turns and they expect you not to be leaning on theirs.

The risk to the car and the stress on the car and driver are much greater in time trials than in autocrossing. The nice, soft, squishable pylons are no longer the most damaging object you can hit. You are shifting often. The reason you have to shift is that you have run out of available engine speed in the lower gears. You will be | *There are real risks* traveling very fast. You will not likely reach | *which must be respected* the top speed of your car, as there are enough turns to slow you down a bit. You will, however, be negotiating some turns at or above 100 mph, and this is more interesting that blasting across a straight road at 145 mph in any case. You have entered an environment where you are putting you and your car at risk. One blown turn can put you into a wall at very high speed, or tumble you down an embankment. Time trialing is not completely berserk, by any means. By careful car preparation and by driving within your limits you will be unlikely to damage the car seriously, and very unlikely to get hurt. However, there are risks and these must always be understood and respected.

Rules differ, but some clubs will allow you to take a passenger along at a time trial. If you are considering time trialing, and have a friend who will give you such a ride, it is a good way to help decide how interested you might be | *Passengers may not be allowed* in doing it yourself. If you become a licensed or certified time trialer, it can be a nice opportunity to share a very intense experience with a friend.

There is a complete chapter (I) devoted to preparing for time trials. What you need for equipment depends on the club with which you are time trialing. A roll bar in the car is often required. You may be required to wear a fire-proof driving suit. Your car will need to have a fire extinguisher on board, within your reach when you are strapped in the car. You will need a five-point safety harness. Usually, you will need two five-point safety harnesses, so an instructor can ride with you.

2. Overall Schedule: Time trials can be run in a single day, but are often run as a weekend event. Saturday will be spent practicing. The first half of Sunday will likely also be spent practicing, with the afternoon devoted to timed runs. Saturday evening may be organized as an informal social event such as a potluck

or barbecue. Since the track is often more than a few minutes drive for the competitors, many people will gather Friday night at a certain motel or camp out at the track in a motorhome, the track car having been towed behind the motorhome on a car trailer.

The technical inspection applied to cars being time trialed is more intense than an autocross technical inspection. In addition to checking everything that is checked at autocross and checking the time-trial-unique requirements such as roll bars, and car numbers, the car will be given a much more thorough going-over. Brake pads will be checked for wear; suspension components will be checked for play; tires must be in better shape. In most clubs, the people doing the job of teching everyone's cars will also be driving their own cars during the event. To give them a chance to drive, tech will usually happen before the event. It may be a few days before the event, or possibly at the track the Friday evening before the event. Some last-minute teching may be done the first morning of the event, before the driving starts.

> *Technical inspection is more intense*

3. Practice Sessions: The practice sessions are where you get most of your track time and can be the most fun part of the weekend. The cars will be divided into groups of 10 to 25 cars or so. The groups are usually named by colors. The basis of the division is lap times so the fastest cars run with each other, separate from the slowest cars which would be in their way. This is also good for the slower cars. Otherwise they would spend all their time letting the faster cars pass. Just because you don't have an extremely fast car does not mean that you can't have a great time at time trials. There is no lack of fun in the slower cars. You do not have to have an Indy car to be challenged by finding the fastest way around the track in your car.

When it gets near the time for your group to go onto the track, you will need to get your car from the pits onto the grid. You will be out there for awhile, and your body will be awash in adrenalin, so a quick stop by the restroom may be in order. When you get to the grid, you need to be in your driving suit (if required, and a good idea even if it is not required), securely belted in and have your helmet on. If you have a camera in the car, get it turned on. Each group will go out onto the track for 15 to 30 minutes, then get off the track to let the next group go out for practice. During the weekend you may get 1.5 to 2 hours of actual time on the track.

During the practice sessions, you are on the track with other cars. These are practice sessions, not racing sessions. If a car catches up with you, you are expected to let it pass, usually by pointing to the side of the car on

> *Passing is not allowed in the turns*

which you wish to be passed. On some tracks there will be straight sections where a driver may pass you without waiting for your signal. Normally, there is no passing in turns. If you find a car behind you that was not there before, you should signal it to pass you at the first opportunity. Even if the car is slower in the corners, and has to use the straight to catch up, or perhaps it is faster in the corners but you always manage to leave it behind in the straights, let it by. The only way it could have caught you is that it is turning faster lap times, and it does no one any good to keep the car behind you.

If you need to pass someone, you should get fairly close to them and slightly to the left, so that you tend to fill the image in their side mirror. When they check their side mirror, they will notice you. When doing this, be careful with cars that may have better brakes, and may be using earlier brake points. Back off as you approach turns that require substantial braking. If you are too close, and they step on those outstanding brakes just a bit early, you may not have room to move to the side. Rear-ending someone would be dangerous, embarrassing and completely your fault.

If you should begin to create safety hazards for other drivers or if you violate the rules of the club with which you are running, you will likely be black-flagged, which means you need to pull in to have a little chat with the chief flagperson.

> *If a car catches up with you, let it pass.*

The chief flagperson will be the one doing most of the talking. Some people bring fairly nice cars to time trials. Believing that they can drive within their limits and bring the car home safely, they will not take it kindly if you are endangering them and their cars. There may be pylons on the track to help you gauge apexes, and entry and exit points, but there is no penalty for hitting them.

In addition to driving within your limits and your car's limits, observing the club rules, such as passing areas, and obeying all the flags, there is a further requirement on you when you are on the track. If you slow down because you have a mechanical problem, or become ill or are leaving the track, you must get your left hand out the window and up, so drivers approaching you from the rear can see that you are intentionally driving slowly and may be exiting the course. They can then plan their immediate line in a safer manner.

During the practice session, drivers or friends who are not on the track may time your laps for you. Using a large board designed to display numbers, they will flash you your time as you go by. You will return the favor when they are running and you are between runs. You will flash only the seconds digit, and maybe a + or - to indicate whether you are high or low in that second. So, a 2:09.72 translates as +09 on the number board.

When you come in from practice you should check your tire pressures, oil level and fuel level, twiddle with suspension if you are into that, then begin thinking about what happened and what you learned. You may want to find out what sort of lap times your competition is running and try to figure out where you can make up the difference between that lap time and your own. If your brakes feel mushy, you should consider bleeding them. You may also want to swap tires if yours are past their useful life, or if it is time to mount that special set that you want to use for the timed laps. A checklist, posted somewhere in or on the car can help you remember everything you need to do at various points in the event. The one illustrated is mine.

After your practice session, you may need to talk to other drivers who were in your practice group. Perhaps someone should have been letting you by, and did not. Perhaps you made some marginal judgments of your own, and need to clarify what you were thinking and exactly how much you expect to reform yourself in future practice sessions. Practice sessions are not wheel-to-wheel racing. Life will be a lot easier if you do your part to keep the communication channels open, and keep the practice sessions friendly.

4. Timed Runs: When it comes time for timed runs, only a very few cars will be on the track at once, usually about three. The flagperson will space you out so you will be unlikely to see any of the other cars. You will get one practice lap to warm up your tires and get into the groove, then one to three timed laps. These are usually timed separately, and you will get to count the best lap as your time.

Beginning of day
unpack
bra on or tape
headlights
air cleaner off
windows down
cold tires 25F,24R

Before each run
bathroom?
gas level?
ear plugs
camera on
mirror position
helmet & gloves on

After each run
PYROMETER
check tires 33/35
oil temperature
camera off
oil level
check gas
talk to other drivers
deal with camera film
clean windshield
sway bar adjustment?

28 TT Checklist

5. General Time Trial Operations: Since this sport involves substantial risk, many aspects of the operation are different from autocrossing. There will be turnworkers at various points around the track. There job is to be the eyes and ears of the chief flagperson all around the track. They will also wave flags as needed, to warn

The turnworkers are the chief flagperson's eyes and ears

you of a dangerous condition ahead (car spun out in the middle of the track, oil on the track), to indicate that your vehicle seems to be having difficulties (smoking, leaking oil, etc.), or to suggest that you need to let the car behind you pass at the next opportunity. There will be an ambulance on site, as well as a tow truck. The reason for all this equipment at the track and in your car is to make the event safer. Cars rarely burn, but they do crash.

6. The Flags: Flags are in use on a road course at start/finish. Additionally, many of the flags are available at turnworker posts around the track. The meaning of the flags is fairly standard, but you should listen carefully when they

Get your hand up when slowing down

are explained at the driver's meeting. Ultimately, the flags mean whatever the people running the event say they mean.

Green Flag: Go or continue.

Checkered Flag: You are done with your practice session or timed runs (whichever you were doing). Continue around the course, use the exit lane near the end of the course and return to your pit area.

Red Flag: This session is stopped right now. Depending upon procedures at the event, you are to stop on the right edge of the track as soon as you see the flag, or you are to continue around the course slowly and pull of the exit lane, returning to the starting grid.

Yellow Flag (standing): There is a problem on the course. Proceed with caution. Do not pass any other cars that are still driving on the track. Also used at the beginning of some practice sessions to give drivers a lap or two of familiarization with the course before passing is allowed.

Yellow Flag (waving): There is a problem in this part of the course. Proceed with extreme caution. Do not pass any other cars that are still driving on the track.

Yellow and Red Striped Flag: A slippery substance (usually oil or water) is on the track. Proceed with caution.

Blue Flag with Diagonal Yellow Stripe: [sometimes a blue flag with a yellow dot] Check your mirrors. There is a car behind you. If it is not someone you just passed, find a place to let the car pass you.

Black Flag: [May be accompanied by a number board displaying your car number.] The officials take exception to some part of your driving behavior. You must use the exit lane and return to the grid for a 'chat'.

Black Flag with Large Red Dot: Your car has a mechanical problem. Get off the line (in case you are spraying oil onto the track you don't want to put it right on the best line), get your hand up, use the track exit and return to the starting grid.

White Flag: Meaning varies a great deal. In some cases the white flag signals the beginning of the last lap of the session. In other cases it means there is an emergency vehicle (tow truck, ambulance or utility truck) on the track. This will normally be the pickup, as conditions requiring a tow truck or ambulance will normally bring out the yellow or red flags.

7. Learning to Time Trial: If you decide to try time trialing for yourself, you will almost certainly have to attend a ground school (classroom) and you likely will have instructors riding with you your first few times. Eventually, you will get a competition license or a time trial certificate from the club sponsoring the series that says you have shown enough skill and judgement to be considered a certified or licensed time trialer. Even with the license, if you time trial at another course or you attend an event with another club, you may be asked to take an instructor for a checkout ride. In some cases this other club may not accept your license at all, and may require that you attend its own school. The schooling will teach you both the general principles of time trialing as well as the particular aspects of the course(s) you will be running.

There is a basic and critically important difference in how you must approach time trialing versus how you approach autocrossing. In autocrossing, it is perfectly

> *Make changes in your approach VERY slowly*

OK to take a chance, and see if the car will negotiate a turn much faster than you have been trying. If the answer is yes, you have made a strong improvement. If the answer is no, then you will be sitting on the course, surrounded by a litter of pylons. In time trialing, pushing beyond what you or your car will do is much more likely to end up with you sitting in the middle of a litter of the parts that used to be your car.

In time trialing, you must make changes in your approach to the course very slowly. If you think you can brake much later going into a turn, first brake just a very little bit later. If you think you can carry lots more speed through a turn, first try to carry just a very little bit more speed.

> *If you're determined to be brave and daring, you should also try to be very lucky*

©1983 Ashleigh Brilliant; Pot-Shot No.4152. Used by permission

Centrifugal force increases with the square of the speed, so increasing your speed from, say, 60 mph to 70 mph (which doesn't really seem like that much a change) in a given turn increases the centrifugal force by 36%. An increase from 60 mph to 75 mph would be a centrifugal force increase of 56%. This will get embarrassing and dangerous rather quickly if you don't happen to have an extra 56% cornering force available. At that point, the exit of the turn takes on a different meaning, and becomes an exit from the course. It is completely impossible to over-emphasize this point: The basic and most important principle in learning to time trial should be that you insist of yourself that you make changes very slowly.

8. The Line versus the Feel of the Car: In addition to staying upright and on the track (a common well-wishing phrase on grid is "Keep the shiny side up!"), there is a further aspect of learning to time trial that needs discussion. This applies, to a certain extent, to autocross as well, but seems much more important for time trial students.

You will find, in the beginning, that the instructors rightly want you to learn the exact line to drive at any given track. This will be greatly emphasized. However, you will not be making sense of the line, because you are not yet driving the car as fast as it will go around the track. You're in

Keep the shiny side up!

the right place, but the suspension isn't yet working as much as it's willing to. In addition to learning the proper line, you must learn how the car feels when it is on that line at speeds approaching the limits of its capabilities for that turn. You can't learn them at exactly the same time. At least, you can't do them both at once yet. If you could drive a proper line at the limits of the car, you would hardly be a student. So, while you learn the line, remember that the line is going to <u>feel</u> different when you get up to competitive speeds.

You will need to find opportunities to feel the car drifting slightly at speeds higher than used in autocrossing before you can begin to approach the limits of the car for a complete lap. On some courses there are turns that are relatively safe, lots of runout room, and nothing to hit. These are the places where you should push the hardest early in your learning (still making small changes!).

One approach you may use, if you believe that you can go faster in a particular turn, is to try to tighten up the exit, not using the entire track. This is NOT something you do frequently, as you normally want to be on the correct line at all times. If you think there is a lot of time left for you in a particular turn, try to end up toward the middle of the track from your proper exit point. If you cannot, or are unwilling, then you are already going as fast as is reasonable with your car on the line you are driving. If you can comfortably end up in the middle of the track, you know you can bring a <u>little</u> <u>more</u> speed with you next time around, and have the car end up at the proper exit point. As always, make such changes very gradually.

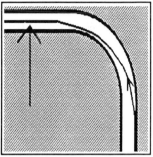

29 Testing Corner Speed

After you have more experience with drifting the car at higher speeds, you will be able to feel when you are at the optimum slip angle for the car and tires, and will not need to try different exits. Once you are at the optimum drift angle, you are going as fast as you can for the line you are driving. If you can't improve the line, then don't bring any more speed into the turn.

Whatever you do, be sure you are trying to learn both the line and the way your car feels at the limit. When you can put both of these together smoothly, you will be doing a pretty good job of driving the car.

9. Time Trial Apexes: The precision with which you drive to the very inside of a turn is more important at time trials than autocrossing, since, in autocrossing, only your lap times are at issue, and, in time trialing, safety is also involved. Be sure that you are intending to get the car to the very inside point of any turn, and that you do what you intend. For any given speed in a turn, this is the safest line. If you miss the apex by two feet, you may find that a turn that was perfectly safe (when you hit the apex) is now impossible for your car to negotiate. If you think you can't get to the apex, turn in anyway. On the faster turns, remember that you will move in to the apex more rapidly than on the slower turns, even though you may still be driving a late apex. If you do end up heading off the track, try to drive off rather than slide off. If you are oversteering when you leave the track, you are probably in for a bit of a spin. Many drivers never exit the track, so don't think that this is a required part of the sport.

> **Hit your apexes, no matter what!**

When you are learning to time trial, be very careful of early apexes. They will be appropriate for certain turns, but an early apex line coupled with aggressive speed may well put you in the position of not being able to negotiate the exit of the turn, at which point you will leave the course. If in doubt, try a later apex. Then, with plenty of laps to practice, you can begin to move the apex point back until you are happy with the line and with the car control.

> **Do *not* use an early apex on a high-speed turn**

You may have had to change your sway-bar settings for time trialing, and this will change the apexes you select and how you drive the turns. A certain level of oversteer tendency at the lower speeds can be quite helpful when autocrossing. Such settings can make the car a vicious handler at high speeds. So you change the sway-bars. Now the car responds differently at the lower speeds. So your approach to the slower turns must change, usually by inducing a certain amount of oversteer through throttle on, throttle lift or more trail-braking. Most street cars set up for high-speed work will need some trail-braking in the slow turns anyway, both to neutralize steering and to make use of the optimum line. Be very wary of inducing any oversteer at higher speeds. You run the risk of unsettling the car greatly.

10. Consistency: Consistent driving is always important to driving success, but it is especially critical that you drive consistently at time trials. If your lap times vary by great amounts, or if the turn feels different each time you go through it, or if you end up entering or exiting turns at different points each time around the track, then your first, second and third priorities must be to become consistent. Only if you can run the course exactly the

> *Only by being able to run the course exactly the same way each time will it become safe for you to approach the limits of the car*

same way each time will it become safe for you to begin to approach driving your car at the limit on a road course. You can't possibly fine-tune your approach by making small intentional changes if you are, at the same time, making large unintentional changes each lap. If you are unable to be sufficiently consistent, then you are much too likely to step over the line that separates what the car will actually do from what it will not do, and you are going to be in the weeds, or worse.

11. Driver Limits Vary Over Time: In autocrossing you will have good days and bad days. On bad days you will hit pylons, have slow times, have the car in the wrong place at the wrong time. The merit in all this is that, when you get your act back together, you will know you have improved.

In time trialing, a 'bad day' should mean nothing worse than slow lap times. Do not push past the point at which you are sure that you have control of the car. You may drive very poorly during the first practice session in your first few events, even though you were doing fine at the end of the weekend the last time you were at this track. When this happens, accept it, get your line under control, stay steady and recognize that you are going to have to work your way back up to your previous level. Additionally, your limits will vary based on your general physical and mental health as well as on the exact current condition of the car and the track.

Track conditions vary a great deal. Just because you turned a 1:55.40 at this track last time you were here does not mean that you are going slowly if the best you can manage today is a 1:57.25. And it certainly does not mean that you just decide to go faster everywhere to get back down to your previous time.

12. Is Time Trialing for You?: There are people who (rightly, to an extent) consider autocrossing sufficiently adventurous and who are vaguely appalled at the idea that anyone would put a nice car onto a road track. On the other hand, driving conditions such as these are, to a degree, the

> *If you really like driving hard, you will really like time trialing*

reason the better sports cars were built. While there are risks, you must balance these with the opportunity to spend a large amount of time driving the car as close to its limit as you care to venture, in an environment that has been made as safe as possible for you. If you really like driving hard, you will really like time trialing.

G. Preparing and Modifying Your Car

Friday night after dinner. There is no doubt in her mind what that means. Time to jack up the car, pull the street wheels and tires, check the brake pad thickness, bleed the brakes and mount that soft set of tires that sticks so well. Probably worth it to check the spark plugs as well. All the while she wonders how much difference the new suspension settings will make . . .

Part 1: Preparing your car

The first part of this chapter covers the steps needed to prepare your car for an event. This may be all you care to know, particularly if you plan to compete in the stock (as opposed to modified) car classes. Some of the steps you may take to modify your car are covered in the second part of the chapter. Don't get too panicked about all the things that people do while modifying perfectly good cars. Many of the modification issues are for the advanced classes, and may not be relevant to you at all. On the other hand, there are some very simple changes you can make to help your driving performance. The additional special preparation needed for time trialing is covered in Chapter I, and the preparation needed for you (including tools and supplies) is covered in Chapter J.

1. Is Competitive Driving Hard on the Car?: In most cases autocrossing is NOT hard on the car. Most of the cars that anyone would bring to an autocross were designed for aggressive driving. (This is not, of course, a sport for the family station wagon, stretch limos or farm pickup trucks.) Autocrossing is hard on the tires and brakes. If you choose to become involved in this sport you will need to come to grips with spending more on these two items than your neighbor, who does not autocross. If you have disc brakes you will find that brake pads are relatively inexpensive and are reasonably easy to replace if you are at all mechanically inclined. Tires will be more expensive, but are a small cost compared to what you spent on the car in the first place.

Time trialing is a bit harder on the car than autocrossing. First, since you spend a great deal more time on the track, and are driving faster during that time, the brakes and tires will show substantially more wear. You are also pushing the engine harder for longer periods of time. This won't be enough to damage an engine in good shape, but it will add wear. Finally, in time trials you practice with other cars on the track. In some cases you follow them pretty closely. Their tires will pick up all the grit on the track and throw it at the front of your car. Because of this, both the paint and the windshield are at risk of becoming pitted. Finally, time trialing involves the risk of an off-course excursion. For some time trialers this never happens. For others it happens more than once. Anytime the car leaves the track it runs the risk of incurring damage, which may be minor or may completely destroy the car.

2. General Preparation: Your car should be well-maintained. This means that it should be serviced no less often than indicated by the owner's manual. The oil should be changed on schedule or more often. A car that is being pushed hard should not have to go much beyond 3000 miles without an oil change, no matter what your owner's manual says.

The brakes, tires, wheel bearings, throttle return springs, belts, and such should be in good working order. The belts should be tensioned correctly; watch for loose belts. The brake fluid should be at a reasonable level. All the tune-up specs should be correct.

Check the tightness of the front wheel bearings. On the lighter cars you can do this by simply pushing and pulling firmly on the top of the front tire. Heavier cars may require that you jack the front end off the ground to see how much play there is in the bearings. Other suspension components should not have excessive play.

The battery needs to be securely mounted, so it doesn't become loose and either create dangerous sparks or spill battery acid. If you can't move it very much by hand, it is probably OK. If moves around very much, find a way to secure it. Otherwise, you will probably fail tech.

3. Oil Level: Check the oil level when the engine is at normal operating temperature. This means your normal operating temperature. Many cars will run noticeably hotter when they go time trialing. Be sure there is enough oil. Most cars should be at, but not above, the full mark. Remember that oil expands with temperature, as much as 10%. If you adjust the oil level when the engine isn't at full temperature, you run the risk of overfilling the motor. Depending on the motor, the results can range from inconvenient to disastrous.

4. Gas: You don't want a full tank of gas in the car when you are making your run, because the extra weight is a disadvantage. A full tank of gas can weigh as much as a passenger, and can slow you down by as much as one second on any given run. As you will soon discover, a second is a lot of time where lap times are concerned. On the other hand, if you have too little gas your car may suffer gas starvation during aggressive cornering. In any case, you can't very well go to an event where you will get many runs and not be able to make all the runs because you have run out of gas. The ideal amount of gas when making a timed run seems to be about 3/8 of a tank. If you determine that your car can run with less gas and still not starve for gas during hard cornering, then you can run with less gas. If you go to an autocross school, you will be doing much more driving than normal so bring about 3/4 of a tank.

You will also need more gas to get through a busy day of time trial practice. Time trialers may spend one or two hours on the track in one practice day, and will use a lot of fuel. For greatest convenience, buy a 5-gallon safety gas can (with a separate funnel, if necessary), and take it with you to the event. Competitive autocrossers sometimes also do this. It allows you to add gas as needed during the day, never running out, never having too much gas, but always having just enough in the car.

5. Get Everything Out of the Car: You will need to unload the car completely when you are at the event. To prepare for this, you may wish to take some of the stuff you normally carry around out of the car before you leave home. In particular, leave any items of exceptional value or exceptional size at home. Check under the seats and remove any odd car parts, fruit, cigarette lighters,

> *Anything loose can become lodged under the brake pedal just when you really NEED the brakes*

soda cans, makeup, whatever. Anything loose can become lodged under the brake pedal just when you really need the brakes. Even if it doesn't get stuck under the pedals, the rattling around can be very distracting when you are trying to concentrate on your driving.

With enough practice you will get pretty good at unloading and reloading the car. One approach that helps with this constant unloading and reloading of the car is an assortment of duffle bags, carrying cases, etc. Amateur and semi-pro musicians soon learn that playing in a band sometimes has a lot more to do with setting up and tearing down equipment and moving it to and from practice sessions and gigs, than it has to do with playing the right chord or a brilliant solo. In the same way, autocrossing and time trialing are a lot about hauling stuff around and loading and unloading it. Grouping your stuff into a few largish packages can make the process a lot more convenient and fast.

You will also need to remove any hubcaps or wheel beauty rings your car might be wearing. They may come loose during aggressive driving, posing dangers to spectators and courseworkers. Some clubs will also require that you remove T-top panels, targa tops and the like.

6. Tires: Tires need to be the right model, the right size, in good condition and at the proper pressure. This is a major topic in solo racing and is the subject of the next chapter.

Check your tire pressure

7. Brakes: Brake pads (or shoes, for drum brakes) should have ample thickness left but should not be brand new. Both rotors and pads (or shoes and drums) take a little time to break in. A week, or so, of normal driving is enough to break in the pads/shoes. The rotors/drums take a bit longer to seat, but are only rarely replaced. Try not to replace any of these parts immediately before an event. If the brake pedal feels soft (spongy) the brake system should be bled to eliminate any gasses trapped in the brake fluid system.

Part 2: Modifying Your Car

This section covers modifications you may wish to make to the car. Some changes are very simple, others may involve a complete restructuring of the suspension system or drive train. The wholesale changes are outside the scope of this book, and there are plenty of good books to help you with such projects. The purpose here is to give you an overview, get you oriented and provide a few tips that may be of help.

8. Deciding What to Change: First, wait until you have enough track experience to know what you want to be different. The tendency to oversteer that you thought was such a vice might be turned into a virtue with a minor suspension adjustment, once you are better at handling the car.

Second, decide how important it is to you that you run in a particular car class. If you are only competing once in a while, or if your pattern is to run just an event or two with several different clubs, then the class rules may not be very important to you. In this case you might as well set up the car in whatever way pleases you. You may not be competitive in any particular class, buy you will still have a lot of fun, and your car will be the way you like it. On the other hand, if you are going to try to attend most of the events of a particular club, and would like to compete for a year-end trophy, or series championship, then you should evaluate the classes carefully.

Third, if car class is important to you, choose a class that suits you, your car and your budget. You are looking for a class into which your car will fit | **Evaluate the car classes carefully** after you have set it up the way you want it. Under most rules, the basic model of the car will restrict it to just a few classes in any given club, the classes ranging from very stock (little or no modification) to extremely modified. So, you will be choosing from these few classes.

Once you have narrowed yourself down to these few classes, read the club rules very carefully and be sure you understand them. You will want to talk to other people in the club driving similar cars to get a better understanding of how key provisions are being interpreted. Watch carefully what these people have done with their own cars. Check with businesses that support competitive modifications. Such businesses are often run by people who know a great deal about what works and what does not.

If you plan to compete with more than one club, you need to be familiar with both sets of rules. Don't be surprised if you find it difficult to place the car cleanly in classes in more than one club. You may find, for example, that a change that leaves you in the showroom stock class in your local RX-7 Club may put you in a very advanced class with SCCA. In each case, the rules are made by groups of people active in the club and, not surprisingly, they often come up with somewhat different ideas about what is a major, performance-enhancing change.

I think it best to start running under stock rules, and progress as you gain proficiency, learn the rules and know that you want to stay with the sport. You are, after all, already familiar with the car and how it drives. As a general rule, the more you modify, the more money it will cost to stay competitive.

If you want to be competitive, you will want to do most of what is allowed in the class in which you are going to run (at least the stuff that seems to help), and be very careful not to do something that will bump you up into the next class. In the long run, the only limits are the rules, the financial costs and your own ingenuity.

9. How Much to Change at Once: Once you decide to make changes, try to take them in small increments, especially in the beginning. By making changes more

gradually, one at a time or so, you can assess the effect of each change, then decide what is the best next step. This also allows you to separate changes in the behavior of the car from improvements in your driving, and it gives you time to get used to one new factor before you have to deal with the next one. When there is a great deal of work to be done to the car to get it into the configuration you desire, such a program is not always possible. It is, however, always worth considering taking the gradual approach.

10. Shock Absorbers: You will want good shocks and you want them to be stiff (have firm valving). Don't go to Sears for this. Koni, Bilstein and Tokico all seem to be good choices. Gas shocks <u>may</u> raise the ride height of the car. If you aren't allowed to lower the car through other means, this may be a real disadvantage, as, in general, you are looking for the lowest practical ride height. Stiffer shocks may act somewhat like stiffer springs, lowering your roll rate.

11. Suspension: The most important performance-affecting part of a solo racer's car is the suspension. There are many changes that can be made to the suspension of your car which will increase its cornering ability. Many seconds can be trimmed from your times by such suspension improvements.

Suspensions are very complex. Before making changes to suspension components or deciding exactly how you want the components adjusted, talk to competitors with your type car. In the bibliography you will find an incredibly good book on suspension tuning by Fred Puhn. Read his book before making suspension changes. Depending on how skilled a mechanic you are, you may consider having the actual work done by someone expert in competition suspension work.

11a. Correcting Suspension Deficiencies: Cars with rear swing axles (such as VW bugs and Corvairs) may be required to install negative camber bars that limit the extent to which the axle may tuck under the car. This is a good modification in any case, as it increases safety.

11b. Deciding What Handling Characteristics are Needed: You will normally be trying to find a compromise between a certain amount of low-speed understeer and some degree of high-speed oversteer. How you resolve the dilemma depends upon the type of events you plan to run and

> *The optimum setup depends upon the driver's skill and preferences*

how you like to drive the car. A car used only for autocrossing should be set up to be neutral or tend toward oversteer at low to medium speeds. Such a setup will often lead to very frightening levels of oversteer at higher speeds, and should be toned down for running time trials.

Therefore, there is not a single 'best' way to set up any given car. The optimum setup will also depend, sometimes strongly, on the skills, preferences and tendencies of the driver of the car. Drivers who are very good at inducing oversteer in low-speed circumstances can set the car up for more natural understeer, and reap the benefits of a more stable car at higher speeds. On the other hand, drivers who insist that the car handle very neutrally at low speeds will find that they must be more careful of some oversteer tendencies at higher speeds.

11c. Tuning the Suspension: Suspensions may be tuned, without changing any components, to achieve certain desired handling characteristics. By using competition-oriented settings for ride height, camber, caster and toe-in the car can be made to stick

> *Many seconds can be trimmed from your time by careful suspension adjustment*

better during aggressive cornering. In some cases the natural tendency of a front-engined car to understeer or a rear-engined car to oversteer can be somewhat counteracted. Your own body weight has an effect on the correct suspension settings. Be sure that suspension tuning is done with something as heavy as you in the driver's seat. You want the car balanced for driving (driver in place), not for parking on the grid.

Competition tuning the suspension usually means lowering the car. The lowered center of gravity will allow your car to corner with less roll and greater speed. Be aware that you may end up with a car that is afraid of no other competitors, but lives in absolute dread of driveways, road dips and speed bumps. Your car may also ride more stiffly after a competition alignment.

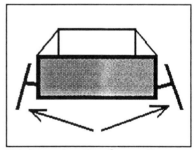

30 *Negative Camber at Rest*

Insofar as possible, the tires will be set for some degree of negative camber. This will splay the bottoms of the tires outward. Thus, when you are hard into a turn, the tire on the outside will not turn under, but rather will sit relatively flat on the track surface, getting a better grip. The two diagrams show these effects, but are quite exaggerated. There are tradeoffs; such suspension tuning will mean that your tires wear out more quickly during normal street driving. The reason they wear out on the street is that you are running on the inside edges when driving straight ahead. Also note that any negative camber in the front of the car will be accentuated when under hard braking, as weight transfers to the front of the car. The weight transfer compresses the front suspension, which, given the way front suspensions are designed, will usually increases camber. None of this is ideal for braking. For this reason less front negative camber is used on cars designed for high-speed (time trial or roadracing) work than on cars set up for autocross. In autocross the cornering ability gained outweighs the small loss in braking effectiveness. If you use your car for both autocrossing and time trialing work, you must reset these adjustments often or live with a compromise between the two ideal points. As will be seen in the next chapter, you can use a pyrometer to

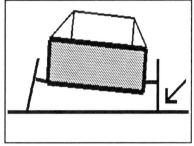

31 Negative Camber at Work

determine the exact amount of negative camber your car wants at the places you drive it.

Large negative camber settings decrease tire life and may be inadvisable for street driving. You get to make your own choices about

> *Your car may dread driveways, sharp dips and speed bumps*

sacrificing tire wear for better lap times, or vice versa.

11d. Sway-bar Adjustment: While you may have a professional set camber, caster and toe-in, the final stiffness adjustment on sway-bars (for those bars that are adjustable) is something you should consider doing yourself. The sway-bars help control the tradeoff between understeer and oversteer; you need to be able adjust them for the actual current conditions if you want optimum performance. The adjusting is not difficult, and it will give you control over a key aspect of the handling of the car. There are many details involved in correctly adjusting a sway-bar, and it is beyond the scope of this book to explain all of these for all possible sway-bars. You should learn how to adjust the ones on your car from a competent suspension professional. Once you have learned, you will find yourself able to do this yourself as you need to.

The function of a sway-bar is to keep the car flat by connecting the two tires at a given end of the car. As the car tries to roll to the outside of a turn, the weight born by the inside tire is transferred to the outside tire. The stiffer the bar is set, the more weight will be transferred. If the bar were perfectly rigid, the body and both wheels would be locked tightly together and would have to move up and down as a unit. Effectively, there would be no independent suspension. However, the bar is constructed as a torsion bar, and, to the extent that it can be twisted, the sides of the car can still move independently. The effort required to twist the bar depends upon several factors. The one you can easily adjust is the exact point at which the wheel (well, suspension component, really) is connected to the bar. By moving this point, either end of the car can be made more stiff.

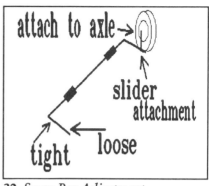

The connections on both sides should be moved the exact same amount when any adjustment is made. Further, as shown, there is a range of adjustment. If you set the slider too tight, suspension travel approaches zero, which will slow down

32 Sway Bar Adjustment

your times, give you a very rough ride, and run the risk of damaging suspension components or the body of the car itself.

The correct adjustment for sway-bars is this: loosen (move toward the cut end) the sway-bar connections on the end of the car that is not sticking well enough, and tighten the sway-bar on the end that is sticking well. The reason that it helps is a tad on the complex side, and is well

> *Loosen the sway bar on the end that is not sticking, tighten the other bar*

explained in Puhn's book. In brief, setting a bar more stiffly means that it will transfer some of the weight at this end that was previously being transferred at the other end of the car. This is done by resisting the roll of the car on the tightened end, before as much weight is transferred on the other end, where the sway-bar is set more loosely. All this happens because of the stiffness of the entire car. If the car does not resist twisting along its long axis, none of this works.

The advantage is this: transferring weight decreases the cornering power of that end of the car, as the extra grip of the heavily weighted tire is less than the grip lost on the lightly weighted tire. So, for example, tightening the front bars will make the front end stick less well, but, since less weight is being transferred at the rear of the car, it will make the rear stick better.

11e. Changing Suspension Components: You may wish to increase the size of the torsion bars, (or install heavier suspension springs) which are the key active part of your suspension. You may also wish to add sway-bars or increase their size. You may also opt for adjustable sway-bars. Increasing the size of these suspension components will certainly give your car a stiffer feeling. If you are making such changes, you should also consider changing the bushings that locate these components from rubber to plastic, which is harder, less deformable and will do a much better job of holding the suspension parts in place. When making your choices, keep in mind that stiffer springs will give your car a much stiffer ride; stiffer sway-bars will be less noticeable, except when cornering. Also remember that all such changes are usually controlled by the car-class rules.

12. Limited-Slip Differentials: Limited-slip differentials, often called Positraction, can help you get power onto the road. The function is fairly straightforward; there is a clutch mechanism in the differential that does not allow one rear wheel to spin very much faster than the other. In competitive driving, there are plenty of times when you will need to apply power while the car is turning. When the car is turning, the outside of the car is supporting more of the weight. This means, in effect, that you have less traction available to the driving wheel on the inside of the car. Without limited-slip, you soon reach a point where all the power you are applying is being used to spin the inside tire, not to accelerate you down the track.

Limited slip will be most useful for cars that have a lot of weight on the front axle. These are normally cars with the motor in the front. Limited-slip <u>can</u> <u>be</u> important even on mid-engined or rear-engined cars.

Note that limited-slip approaches are almost never used on front-wheel drive cars, or on the front end of four-wheel drive cars. On such cars, when one front wheel loses traction, the wheel that does not lose traction will exert enough force to pry the steering wheel loose from the driver's hands, and cause an abrupt turning of the car.

13. Modifying the Controls: You interact with your car through various instruments and controls, such as throttle pedal, brake pedal, steering wheel and gearshift lever. All controls should be convenient, so you can spend your energy concentrating on the challenge of driving your very best.

13a. Seating: Proper seating position is extremely important. If you have a choice, select seats that put you in a comfortable position, and that give you lateral support. Lateral support means that the seat supports you at your sides, as well as below and beneath you. Some seats are constructed so that you sit <u>into</u> them. The

> *Seats with lateral support are <u>very</u> helpful*

back curves around you, and the bottom of the seat comes up on the sides. Such seats help you stay well located. Good seatbelts can also help. A four-point harness, not needed for safety in autocrossing, can still be of value in helping you stay firmly in your seat. Finally, if there isn't a good place to rest your left foot, construct one. You need the left foot pressed firmly down on something to help stabilize you body in the seat.

13b. The Steering Wheel: You should evaluate your current steering wheel to decide if another will work better. The wheel should be relatively small in diameter, so you don't have to move your arms all over the car to move the steering wheel. The wheel itself should fit nicely in your hand, probably be a bit fatter than what you might consider normal. The wheel should support comfortable hand grips at 9:00 and 3:00. Momo makes comfortable wheels for a variety of cars.

13c. The Shifter: The shift knob should be well at hand and comfortable. If you have to stretch to reach the shifter, or if it is in your way when you don't need it, then something needs to change. The most common problem seems to afflict tall people who must move the seat fairly far back. Once you are sitting so far back, the shifter may seem too far forward. Often the shifter position will be adjustable, with a little bit of work. For some cars, you may find aftermarket (or factory) short-shift kits that will lessen the travel required from one gear to another. If you just need more length on the shift lever, you may be able to find an aftermarket shift knob that will effectively extend the shifter. Failing this, you can, through welding, add or subtract shift lever length.

13d. Throttle Block: You may wish to alter the geometry of your throttle pedal to help you with heel and toe work. The easiest way is to attach a block of wood to the throttle pedal. In addition to raising the level of the throttle pedal to make it more accessible under braking, the left edge can be extended a bit toward the brake pedal, so the right foot doesn't have to stretch quite so far. If you do this, be <u>very</u> careful that you don't find yourself accidentally pushing down on the throttle when all you are trying to do is apply the brakes. Additionally, if you run time trial

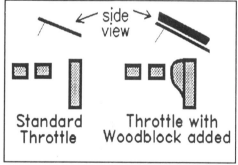

33 Wood Block on the Throttle

events or actual races, you may find that the level of the brake pedal gets lower and lower during a 30-minute practice session or during a race. After the brake pedal gets sufficiently low, heel and toe turns into something more like ankle and toe. If you add the block of wood, be sure you have designed it to work acceptably even when the brakes are very low.

13e. Instruments: Your car talks to you through the sounds it makes, the motions it makes, sometimes the smells it makes, and through the instruments. You need to be able to see the instruments clearly and quickly. The tachometer is one of the most important of these. If you can, rotate the tachometer so the maximum engine rpms (red-line) is at about 1:00 of a clock face. This way, since you will normally be driving with the engine operating at high rpms, when you glance at the tach you will be able to glance at the top (12:00) portion of the tach and see the needle right away.

You may wish to install additional gauges if your car relies mostly on warning lights. Oil pressure and water temperature are the most important. For time trialing you should have both an oil gauge and a VERY BIG oil pressure warning light. Most drivers don't watch the oil gauge closely enough, with all the intense driving, other cars and tachometer requiring so much attention. You will want to know if the oil pressure drops dangerously, and the BIG oil light will do this.

13f. g-analyst: The g-analyst is a novel instrument that you can mount in your car. It measures lateral acceleration (acceleration, braking and turning) as you drive and records eight minutes of this information electronically. The controls function more or less like a tape recorder, allowing you to play back information on the built-in display screen. If you record an autocross run, or a few laps of a time trial practice, you can then see whether you are smooth and aggressive in transitioning from brakes to turning, turning to throttle, etc. There is also an interface that allows you to use a personal computer printer to print the information. As of this writing, the g-analyst is priced at a little less than $400.

The g-analyst is a good tool for the intermediate driver who wishes to learn everything as quickly as possible. The novice competitive driver has many basic skills and techniques to learn, and the usefulness of the g-analyst may well be overshadowed by the confusion added. It is one more thing requiring energy and attention. For the driver who has become truly expert, it may be an interesting toy, and it may provide some useful feedback, but it should not be of overwhelming value. However, those drivers who lie between these two extremes may profit greatly. In particular, two drivers may compare the charts for the same course and find out who is smoother and faster in each part of the course. If you really want a calibration, run a chart on yourself, then ask a really good driver to run the course, and chart that. If that driver turns in a better time, comparing the two charts will quickly tell you whether you are simply having specific problems with some particular parts of the course, or whether you are losing a small amount of time on most parts of the course. Phone the manufacturers, Valentine Research, at 800-331-3030 or 513-984-8900 if you want further information on this.

14. Chip Substitution: The general topic of engine modification and performance tuning is left to you, your mechanic, your shop manual and the

people who specialize in such work. However, one modification can be made quite easily to many modern cars and it deserves a mention.

The engines of many of the newer cars are controlled by an electronic brain. Alternate computer chips are available for some of these cars; the chips modify the way the engine responds to various conditions, and usually allow the engine to produce more horsepower. In some cases you don't get the maximum effect unless you also remove the catalytic converter, making the car illegal for street use in most states. You may also find that taking the catalytic converter off without changing the chip leads to very bad results.

In the past, changing the computer chip usually has been considered a big-time modification that would bump your car up one or more classes. In some areas the mood is shifting a bit, and changing the chip is treated more like tuning the carburetors or the fuel injection system. Consult your local rules before making changes of this type.

Be sure that you are dealing with people who know what they are doing and have a good track record (as it were) in this field. Just because someone is willing to sell you a chip does not mean that they have done a proper job of engineering the chip. A casual approach, or one driven more by marketing considerations than technical expertise, can quickly do major damage to your motor. Be sure that you have an absolute right to return the chip if you find it unsatisfactory. Then, when you get the chip, test the car with the new chip and the stock chip, and make your own choice whether the new chip is an improvement.

15. Power Steering: The very rapid steering required during competitive driving, especially during autocrossing, are more than some power steering units can handle. The cars most afflicted by this are mostly from the '60s. By using a very small restriction at the output of the power steering pump, the designers of that era created a system that would work very well in normal driving at low rpm. Unfortunately, they sacrificed some responsiveness during very aggressive driving. On such cars steering boost essentially goes away and steering effort increases dramatically during very quick turning. The solution is to enlarge the pump output restrictor. On Corvettes it should be bored out to about .150". If you need to have this done, have it done by someone who is familiar with the problem.

H. Tires

He surveys the grid area. Nothing very new, save some fairly interesting machinery making first appearances today, and a few new faces. Somehow all the air equipment seems to stand out from the picture. Tires everywhere, of course. But he sees what must be thousands of air pressure gauges: on dashboards, on passenger seats, on top of cars, hanging out of blue jean pockets. A few people are inflating tires up with cigarette-lighter-powered pumps. And everywhere, the red air tanks, waiting patiently for their moment of glorious usefulness. Sometimes this group seems a lot more like an incredibly mobile army of tire inflators than a group of competitors.

Tires are the links between your car and the track. Your most valiant efforts to improve the car and your own driving skill may yield poor results if you have not made sure that your tires are the right ones and are doing all they can to help you. Managing your tires may be as straightforward as setting the pressure to a reasonable value, or as complex as using a tire pyrometer to tune your suspension. The basic issues with tires are choosing the tire size, brand and style, choosing a pressure, and setting that pressure.

1. Tire Pressures Vary: A given volume of air in a tire will vary in pressure, depending on the temperature. If you don't have a leak in the tire, changing the temperature will change the pressure. So, we need to ask ourselves, what will change the temperature of the tire? Certainly a thirty-minute time trial practice session, cornering at the limit will increase the temperature of the tires. Even an autocross run will change the temperature, as the tires are subjected to cornering and braking forces. Sitting in the hot sun will also change the tire temperature.

You really don't care what pressure the tires have when they are sitting on the grid. You care about the pressure when the tires are operating on the course. You can easily check and adjust the

> *The only important tire pressure is the operating pressure on the course*

pressure immediately after you get off the course. Unless the track conditions change (sun heating the pavement, major weather change or some such), tires that were adjusted after the previous run should be OK for the next run. The pressure check when you have just completed a run is the most important tire-pressure adjustment.

There <u>will</u> be times when it is pretty important to have the tire pressure quite correct for the first run. In some autocross events you may only get two runs. You will probably run better the second run, after you have seen the course, but you still want that first run to be as good as possible.

In such cases, you have to have a reasonable idea of how much the pressure will increase during your run. If the tires have been sun-baked (black tires sitting in the sun can get quite hot), they may not increase temperature very much during a run. The air rushing by will tend to cool them, while your cornering and braking will tend to heat them. If the tires have been sitting in the shade, and are now heading out onto a very hot, sun-baked track, you can guess that they will heat up more. Pressure growth of 2-4 pounds is typical in autocrossing, but will vary depending on the starting temperature, the temperature of the track surface, and the extent to which you are sliding. Pressure growth of 8 pounds during a time trial practice session is normal. Pressure growth will also be greater on the side of the car that is on the outside for most of the turns. If you are running clockwise (as seen from above), the left-side tires will increase in pressure somewhat more than the right-side tires. If you need to try to get the tires just right for that first run, take the specific conditions into account as you hunch how much the pressure will increase.

In time trialing, it takes one to two laps for the tires to come up to a reasonably stable temperature. What you need for a timed run is the amount of air that will get the pressure right as you begin your timed lap(s). If, during practice, the tires don't feel right until the end of the second lap, you may need to increase the amount of air for timed laps.

2. Checking Tire Pressure: Step one in checking the tire pressure is being sure that you have a good tire gauge that is in good calibration. The most accurate and easy to use tire gauges are sold at better automotive supply stores and racing supply | *Calibrate the air gauge* | stores. They have a gauge that you can hold in your hand, and a tube leading to the nozzle that is placed on the valve stem. There will also be a small button that will allow you to bleed air from the tire, reducing the pressure. Routinely check your gauge against other gauges at the track. If you find a big difference between your gauge and several others, replace the gauge. More than one autocross has been lost because someone's gauge went sour.

If you will get several autocross runs, take the first run with slightly more air than you expect to need. (If you are used to checking the tires hot, this <u>does</u> <u>not</u> mean slightly more <u>pressure</u>. It means that you set the cold pressure so the tires, <u>once</u> <u>hot</u> will have just a bit more pressure than you want.) Then, after the run, you can bleed the tire down to the proper pressure. Once you have done this, you should be able to leave the tires alone unless conditions change.

On any given day, once you have checked the tires immediately after a run, don't even consider checking them cold. You can check them after each run, if you wish, but, unless you have a leak somewhere, they shouldn't change much <u>when</u> <u>hot</u>. If the course surface is getting hotter, some of this will transfer to your tires and you may have to bleed out a little air after runs later in the day. Remember, there are far too many variables when the car is sitting. If the temperature drops, the pressure <u>has</u> to drop. Such is the physical and moral responsibility of the tire. Once you are on the course again, the tires will get hot. If they were right after your last run, they are as well-checked as they are going to get.

<u>3. Selecting the Desired Tire Pressure</u>: The correct tire pressure is important both for performance and for safety. Aggressive cornering often requires more pressure to keep the tires from rolling over onto their shoulders (the additional pressure helps keep them upright). Even if rollover is not an issue, a given tire on a given car will operate best at a certain pressure. Your job, as driver and chief racing maintenance technician, is to determine what that pressure is.

The correct pressure will depend on the tire brand, size and style, the weight of your car, the suspension settings you are using and the feel you like from your tires. In general, you will want higher pressures than the manufacturer's recommended settings. <u>35-42 pounds of pressure when the tire is hot (has just</u> <u>completed a run) is a good starting point</u>, if you have nothing else to go on. Check with other people driving a similar car with similar equipment. It's usually not so competitive at the events that people won't share with you some of their secrets and opinions. Selecting the ideal pressure to run takes trial and error (lots of both).

Once you have selected a starting point, try pressures higher or lower by about five pounds. For time trialing, you get enough laps each practice session that you can simply try a different pressure for a session, and see how your best lap times compare. Be sure that you leave yourself more than normal room for error when testing tire pressures, as you may find that the pressure you are testing doesn't work as well as you would have expected. For autocrossing, it is best to try different pressures at events where you get a lot of runs. That way you can settle down with the course, and get to where your times for each run are pretty consistent. Only then will you have much of an idea whether a different pressure can help. You cannot rely merely on how the car feels. Higher pressures often

feel more precise and controllable, but yield slower lap times than lower
pressures, which may feel mushy.

If you find a big jump in pressure helps (whether jumping to less pressure or
more pressure), try another big jump. Do this as long as performance improves.
When things stop improving, go back to the pressures that seemed to work the
best, and begin fine tuning. Listen to what others have to say, but rely on your
own judgement about tire pressures.

On the West Coast, about three years ago, it was very popular to run Yokohama
008R tires at relatively high pressures, as much as 44 pounds when the tire was
hot. However, pyrometer
work (more about
pyrometers in a moment)
during time trials with these
tires showed that much

> *Up to a point, lower pressures seem to allow the tire to grab better, but the car will feel more mushy, less precise*

lower pressures (as low as 30 pounds hot) worked better. In the last two years
most people have lowered their normal tire pressures on these tires and had good
success. Careful pyrometer work will usually tell you what is going on.

Competition tires may perform <u>reasonably</u> well over the range from about 30
pounds to about 45 pounds. The optimal pressure will vary by car type, specific
car and driver preference. The higher pressures tend to produce a predictable
feeling to the car, but there is a certain sense of an over-eagerness to begin sliding,
a 'skatey' feeling; the higher the pressure, the greater this sensation. The lower
pressures seem to allow the tire to grab a bit better, but the car will feel a little
more mushy, less precise. If the tire pressures are too low, of course, you will be
rolling the tire too far over onto the shoulder.

4. Checking Tire Rollover: In selecting the pressures
you prefer, be sure to watch the shoulders of the tires.
If you are running pressures so low that the tire is
rolling over excessively (substantial scuffing of the
sidewall beyond the tread area) you are running a
serious risk of the tire not being able to rebound into
its normal shape. You are also running a risk of going
too slowly, as under-inflated tires will not give you
the best lap times.

Starting at the tread and continuing around the
shoulder and possibly proceeding just a little bit up
the sidewall, you will see scuffing that has the same
general dull appearance as the tread portion of the
tire. This should not extend past the shoulder of the   **34 *Marking for Rollover***

tire. If it does, it means the tire is rolling over too far to be effective, and decreasing your traction. You may also be in danger of a sudden loss of air pressure if you have the tire very soft and roll it too far. Note that checking for scuffing may not tell you when you are too high in pressure, as even tires with substantial pressure will roll over to some degree.

If this isn't your first event (or hard cornering) on these tires, you may not be sure whether the scuffing you see is a result of today's runs or some previous event. An easy way to find out exactly how far your tires are rolling over today is to mark the tires with white shoe polish. After your run, there will be polish left at the point where the scuffing stops.

Some people try to fine tune tire pressures by measuring rollover. There are rules of thumb, such as 3 pounds of pressure added to the tire will decrease rollover by .25". Be extremely wary of such generalizations. How much tire roll changes with pressure may vary at different pressures, and will certainly be a function of the general tire design

> *Focusing on tire rollover may confuse improper inflation with camber misadjustment*

and sidewall stiffness. More important, too much rollover may indicate insufficient negative camber. If camber is adjustable, be sure it is right before wandering too far away from reasonable tire pressures. Also remember, lap times and pyrometer work will give you better information than tire rollover. The most important part of checking tire rollover is to be sure you aren't rolling over too far.

5. Adjusting Car Handling Characteristics with Tire Pressure: It used to be common for drivers to raise the tire pressure, by 4 pounds or so, at the end of the car that was sliding too much or too soon. If your tires stick better at a higher pressure, this might be of some advantage, but, then, why were you not already running them at the pressure they like the best? The better approach is to find the pressure your tires like best (when on your car) and leave them there. If you need to compensate by altering your driving technique, inducing more oversteer in certain cases, or less in other cases, you can do this knowing that all four tires are set up to stick as well as they possibly can.

As a last resort, if you are unable to make any other handling adjustments, and are having a problem with massive understeer or oversteer, you might decide to change the pressure on the end of the car that is sticking too well, to make it stick less well and make the car handle more neutrally. You will give up some capability

> *Find the best tire pressure and stick with it*

with this approach, as there will be some cases when you need the extra stickiness you have given up, so this is only for desperate cases. In general, non-optimal pressure on the driving axle will impede acceleration, non-optimal pressure in the front will impede braking and slow-speed turns, and non-optimal pressure in the rear will impede high-speed stability.

6. Pyrometers: Pyrometers are instruments for measuring temperature, particularly temperatures above ambient (normal air temperature). Some pyrometers are built with special tips for testing tire temperatures. The use of pyrometers is relatively common in time trials and road-racing. It is also used with autocrossing, but your measurement technique has to be very precise, as tires often do not get completely hot in one autocross run. The basics are this: the part of the tire that is the hottest is the part that is working too hard.

Using a tire pyrometer, each tire is measured in three spots, all IN the tread: the outside rib, the middle rib and the inside rib. The tires must be measured immediately after the car finishes the run, since temperatures will start to drop and to equalize across the tire as soon as the car is no longer being driven aggressively. Immediately means that you have someone waiting for you with the pyrometer, and, as soon as you get off the course, you jump out of the car and begin taking readings. The recording form will clarify how to interpret the readings. Basically, if one edge of the tire is hotter than the other, that edge is doing too much work and the camber needs to be changed toward the other side. If the middle of the tire is hotter than the edges, it is carrying too much pressure (converse if it is lower in temperature than the edges). If one end of the car is noticeably hotter than the other, then it is sliding (or operating at higher slip angles) more than the other end, and the appropriate sway-bar adjustments need to be made.

Obviously, driving technique is related to the question of oversteer and understeer, especially oversteer. If you use a tire pyrometer after the car has been driven by drivers with different approaches, you will get very different answers about what sorts of adjustments the car needs.

7. Tire Selection & Preparation: There are several factors to consider when deciding when to buy tires and which tires to buy. The best first approach is to be very aware of what seems to be working for your type of car. Look at the tires on the cars of the drivers who are winning.

All tires make compromises between performance on a dry surface and performance on a wet surface. Additionally, all tires must reach a compromise between stickiness and long life. Finally, each tire company has somewhat differing theories about

Most slicks are useless in the wet

proper rubber compound formulation, tread design and case design (especially

Tire Pyrometer Readings

Date: _____   Time: _____   Location: _____

TIRE PRESSURES: Ambient Temperature: _____

LF   RF   Track Surface: _____

Cold Hot   Hot Cold   Slow Speed Handling: _____

| C | H | | H | C | High Speed Handling: _____

| C | H | | H | C | On actual laps, proportion
                        of oversteer to understeer: _____
LR   RR

Front of Car

Left Front   Right Front   Front/Rear
                                          range should
| | | | | | | | | | | | be 20˚ to 40˚.
                                          Loosen the sway
                                          bar at hot
| | | | | | | | | | | | end; tighten
                                          at other end.
Left Rear   Right Rear

Use whole patch;   Middle reading should
20˚ to 40˚ range OK.   equal average of the
Adjust camber away   outside readings.
from hot side.   Lower the pressure if middle
                              temp is too high; raise
                              pressure if middle temp
                              is low.
Measure ribs, not grooves.
Ideal temperature = 200˚ ± 20˚

35 Pyrometer Chart

sidewall stiffness). Keeping in mind that there are <u>many</u> variables, we can
imagine four basic types of tires: <u>street tires</u>, which have plenty of tread depth,
relatively hard rubber, and are designed to last a long time and perform
adequately well on wet surfaces; <u>competition tires</u>, which have some tread, softer
rubber, will run for a few thousand miles on the street, or perhaps a season of
racing, and which are often only barely adequate in wet conditions; <u>advanced
competition tires</u>, which have even less tread, softer rubber, and may last for as
few as 10 autocross runs; and <u>racing slicks</u>, which have no tread pattern, very soft

rubber, won't last very many miles (but may well last longer than advanced competition tires), stick very well under dry conditions and are, usually, unmitigated disasters on a wet surface.

If you are a beginning solo racer, you probably are not going to be in a class that allows racing slicks. Your best choice is among the competition tires, which includes such brands as Yokohama, B.F.Goodrich, Goodyear and Mickey Thompson. Hoosiers, though

> *Some tires must be shaved in order to perform to their maximum potential*

treaded, are sometimes treated as race tires (slicks) and not allowed in the stock classes. Watch what other people in your area are using to win, and watch for comprehensive tire tests in automotive magazines. The tire situation changes from year to year.

Be a little cautious about advertisements that claim one company or another has won most of the classes at a competitive event. The tires chosen by national champions may be from the group of advanced competition tires, unsuitable for your interests and budget. Also, sponsorship and incentives may influence the tire choices of serious racers (though no serious racer would run very long on tires that are not competitive).

Tires need shallow tread to perform to their maximum potential. If you buy tires with a lot of tread depth, then they must be shaved to perform their very best. Shaving is the process of stripping off some portion of the tread. This gives the tire a bit more lateral stiffness, as the reduced-height tread blocks will not distort to the side as easily. The tire will stick better and be more predictable.

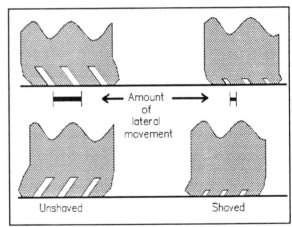

36 Tread Squish

The impact of shaving seems to depend upon the brand of tire. Some treaded tires designed for competition are manufactured with very shallow tread and do not need shaving. Other tires will fall apart (chunk) when pushed very hard in a non-shaved condition, but perform admirably when shaved. It is best to talk to people who are running your chosen tire to see what seems to be the best approach. If you are <u>very</u> serious about a particular event, you might want to shave a new set down to 3/32" tread depth. Of course, one weekend with several runs (or practice sessions) is about all you'll get out of tires shaved so far down.

If you get very serious about the sport you should pay attention to the tire manufacturers who offer a modest amount of cash if your car wears their stickers and you win on their tires.

Some classes allow the use of racing slicks. Racing slicks stick very well, and can be a lot of fun. If you end up running slicks on your autocross car, remember that they are designed to work when hot, and you will have a difficult time getting them hot in one autocross run. Additionally, you normally must make major modifications in your suspension to take advantage of the increased stickiness of such tires.

8. When to Replace the Tires: Unless you have a very large racing budget, choosing when to replace tires may be more difficult than choosing whether or not to shave them. Street tires have wear bars, which will tell you when the Department of Transportation thinks you should replace the tires. These are small sections of the groove of the tire that are just a little bit less deep than the rest of the

> *Some tires wear out*
> *BEFORE the tread is gone*

groove. Once you have worn the tire down enough, you aren't quite down to the bottom of the groove in most places, but you will be down to the wear bars. At this point your tread looks like it spans across the groove. In most states you cannot legally drive on the street with tires that are worn past the wear bars.

For competition purposes, some tires become useless and worn out before the tread is gone. Sometimes this happens long before the tread is gone, even if the tires were originally shaved. The experience is simply that the tires stop sticking as well as they have been doing. Several theories try to explain the factors that govern this tire behavior:

● The number of heat cycles theory claims that each time the tires are heated by competitive driving and then cool down, they age one heat cycle. After a certain number of heat cycles, the rubber compound stops working as well.

● The hours at temperature theory suggests that a tire has the ability to sustain only a certain number of elapsed minutes at competitive temperatures. After this time, the tires will no longer work well. One proponent of this theory claims that Yokohama 008R tires stay good for about 100 minutes at temperature.

● The time since heated theory claims that, once a tire is brought to competitive temperatures, it loses or transforms part of the important chemical structure, and continues to age rapidly from that point forward. By this theory, a tire that was used just once or twice, then left to sit for a year or so, would likely be of no further use. You can certainly see this to be true for yourself by looking at tires that have been used then left to sit; they seem old and hard. It could be that skimming off a bit of the tread surface would restore performance.

One caution: Despite theories 1 & 2, it does appear that <u>some</u> tires need a few runs to get scrubbed in. Until they are scrubbed in, they will feel a little slicker and more squirrely. If you own such tires, don't make a very important run on tires that have never been on pavement.

It is likely that all these theories are operating to some degree. The only useful conclusions to draw from all of this are the obvious ones: the very best set of tires for any given run is freshly shaved tires that have just barely been scrubbed in. The very worst tire is one that was never shaved, is old, has been heat cycled many times and is now low on tread. Shave tires if you can afford to get less life out of a set. When you sense that the tires are no longer sticking as they once did, and the problem is not a slippery track surface, it's time to replace them.

9. <u>Wheels and Spacers</u>: The most important aspect of dealing with wheels it to be sure to torque the lug nuts properly. Find out the proper torque for the lug nuts for your wheel. If they are stock wheels, then your local service department should know. If they are aftermarket wheels, call the

> *Torque the lug nuts!*

manufacturer and find out. Then, carry a torque wrench and make sure that the lug nuts are properly torqued every time they've been off the car. Because of the expansion and contraction that is a natural part of wheels getting hot on the track, many time trialers (and racers) check lug nut torque before each session on the track. You will get a more precise reading if you keep the threads of the lug studs lubricated with grease.

Tire size, wheel diameter and wheel width are often limited by the rules of the class in which you are running. You will find it a competitive advantage to run the widest wheels allowed, as long as you can get them under your fenders. Even with the same tire, a wider wheel will support the tire sidewall better

> *Keep the weight of the wheel to an absolute minimum*

under aggressive cornering. When you buy the wheel, be sure to measure the width and offset very carefully to avoid running illegally and getting protested. You should also be conscious of keeping the weight of the wheel to an absolute minimum. Wheels are unsprung weight, which means that they have to operate below the level at which your suspension can help. The less unsprung weight, the better.

If your class allows more than one specified wheel diameter, you may decide that you want to run the smaller diameter wheel. This is helpful if your car is too far down in its rev range when you are trying to accelerate out of turns, as the smaller wheel will lower the overall gearing of the car. It will also lower your car without changing the suspension geometries by a great deal.

Do not buy cheap wheels. Be sure your wheels are strong and light. Don't use widened steel wheels. They are heavy, have too much flex and are somewhat prone to failure. It is not worth taking any risks with wheels. If they fail, you can bet it won't be when they are sitting in the garage; it will be in the middle of severe cornering or on high-speed bumps.

You may be allowed to run spacers, which sit between the wheel and the flange on which the studs or bolt holes are mounted. This effectively increases the track width of your car, and is a generally good idea. Use only the full-circle, one-piece spacers. Anything else may not offer a perfectly flat surface. If the wheel is bolted tightly to an irregular surface, there will be a great deal of stress in the wheel, possibly leading to stress-fracture and wheel failure. If you use spacers, you also need to be sure that your lug nuts have a good grip on the stud (or, conversely, that the wheel bolts still engage in the holes a sufficient depth). The area of contact between the stud and the nut should be at least 1.5 times the diameter of the stud. You may have to mount longer studs or find longer bolts to achieve this.

10. How Many Sets of Tires and Wheels: In the very beginning, you can simply drive to the event and run on your normal tires. This is especially true for autocrossing. (In time trials, your tire needs to be rated for the speeds you will be driving, and should be at least a competition-oriented tire.) However, you will soon grow to resent the extent to which your normal street tires prevent you from getting your lap times down into the range you want. Presuming that the car you are using for solo racing is also one you drive on the street, you are now in a bit of a quandary. Should you simply run competition tires on the car all the time? Or, should you buy an extra set of wheels, so you can have two sets of tires, one for regular street use and one for competition?

Few people will wish to run competition tires on the street all the time. They are expensive, won't last terribly long, and won't perform very well in wet conditions. The only advantage is that the car will <u>always</u> be handling its very best (except when there is rain!), allowing you an extra margin of safety and the ability to drive the same car on the course as you drive every day.

If you want two sets of tires, you need a second set of wheels. You also need to change to the competition tires before each event, and change back to the normal street tires after the event. You will see many people changing tires at the event.

This is a perfectly reasonable choice if you compete on racing slicks or advanced competition tires, neither of which may be legal on the street and neither of which will last very long on the street. If your competition tires are not super soft, and the event is less than 100 miles away, it makes more sense to change the tires in the comfort of your own garage. A few highway miles will not put nearly as

> *An extra set of tires means an extra set of wheels*

much wear on the tires as a couple of aggressive laps on the course, and you don't have to haul the tires and floor jack (much more convenient than the jack that came with your car) to the event. You may also use the tire changing ritual as an excuse to buy that air compressor you've always wanted, since an air-powered impact wrench makes quick work of changing a set of tires.

For time trialing you may quickly get back into the drill of taking the jack and a second set of tires to the event. If you get much practice time, you may want to practice on a set of tires that is not ideal, and save a set that is shaved and broken in just right for your timed laps.

11. Nitrogen in the Tires?: You may hear someone tell you that you should run nitrogen in your tires to reduce the amount of pressure increase as the tire gets hot. I can find no justification for this. Nitrogen, like all gases, follows the ideal gas law, which states that temperature and pressure (given a constant volume) are directly

> *Nitrogen will not reduce pressure growth*

proportional. So, if nitrogen gets hot, it will expand. Since it has about the same specific heat as oxygen, it will get as hot. Air is about 80% nitrogen in any case. Nitrogen is also extremely inconvenient to carry around.

I. Preparing Your Car for Time Trials

Carefully, he removes the roll bar from the garage wall and inspects it. The padding is still in good shape; the fire extinguisher and camera mount are secure. He slides it into the convertible from the top, careful not to scratch the paint or tear the leather. Following a carefully-learned sequence he gets the allen bolts started, then, when they are all located, tightens them firmly with the newly-purchased air-ratchet. There's always a little tension as he prepares this fine car for track-play time. It would be criminal to stuff the car into a wall. Yet, exploring performance limits seems to be what the car was built to do, and he secretly harbors a fantasy that the car must be glad to be owned by someone who will go to all this effort so it can go out to the big track to play.

This chapter is devoted to the special preparation that you and your car may need to go time trialing (SCCA Solo-I). Remember that you are asking your car to act like a race car; it will be exposed to racing hazards and stresses. Do not assume anything!

There are four general types of preparation needed for time trialing: required safety items such as harnesses and rollbars, other club-specific requirements (car numbers, for example), modifications made to make the car more reliable and modifications/equipment to increase performance. The topics will be covered in that order. Remember that there are elaborate rules governing car modification. In some cases certain modifications are either required or prohibited for safety reasons. In other cases, certain performance-enhancing modifications result in a change of class. Be sure to review your rule books before making any changes, so you know what the consequences will be.

1. Driving Suit: Most clubs require that you wear a fireproof driving suit. This usually can be either a one-piece jumpsuit, or a two-piece suit. The one-piece approach seems to offer a bit more real protection in case of fire, but, when you are not driving, you will spend hot weekends walking around with the top half of the suit tied around your waist. When driving suits are required you will also need fireproof gloves and socks. You may also have to wear a balaclava (headsock) to protect your face in case of fire. Fires are extremely rare in time

trials, but, when one of these suits is needed, it is <u>really</u> needed. Specific shoe requirements may not exist (well, you <u>will</u> have to wear shoes), may be that the shoes must have non-synthetic uppers, or may specify fireproof driving shoes.

When choosing a driving suit, err on the side of letting it be too loose. You want it comfortable while driving, not stylish while walking around the pits. Many racing supply shops have suits for rent, allowing you to avoid the cost of a suit until you are sure you want to continue with this sport. When it does comes time to buy a suit, you can get one custom built (measurements, choice of material color and trim style) for not much more than the ones on the rack.

2. <u>Safety Harness</u>: You will almost certainly be required to install a five-point safety harness in the car. This is an elaborate seatbelt system that includes a lap belt, belts over each shoulder, and an anti-submarine belt heading from your navel to the floor, to keep you from sliding out underneath the lap belt in case of a frontal collision with some object that your car finds difficult to move. The straps will be 2" or 3" high-strength material. The release mechanism will operate very easily. All anchor points will have to be latched and secured with a cotter key. In most cars you can find reasonable places to mount the lap belt and the anti-submarine belt. The shoulder belts are normally attached to the roll bar. Do <u>not</u> attach the shoulder belts to the floor behind the driver's seat. Such a configuration can lead to compression of the spine in a severe impact. Be sure to wear the lap belt down low over your hips. Otherwise, a strong impact is more likely to give you internal injuries.

3. <u>Roll Bar</u>: Club rules differ, but many require a roll bar in every car. In some cases only the more rowdy, highly modified cars must have a roll bar. In all cases, convertible and open cars must use roll bars. SCCA specific roll bar design requirements are the most widespread. If your bar meets their technical requirements, it will probably be acceptable anywhere.

Bolt-in bars are available for many cars at your local competition shop. Having a bar custom made for your car will be more expensive, but may allow a more convenient fit allowing you better use of the interior. A roll bar can be installed in most cars with very | *Pad the roll bar* | minimal disruption, and some can be removed. Normally, it will be easier to find one that you can live with, and leave it in the car. In most cases you will be required to add thick, high-impact foam padding over the roll bar anywhere a driver or passenger might bump into the bar in case of an accident. This is very good to do, even if it isn't required.

If you are going to install a roll bar, you may, depending on the nature of the car and your use of it, wish to go a step further and install a full cage. A cage is a structure built like a roll bar, but extending around the entire driver's area, with bars across the top of the side windows and windshield, and extending down the front pillars to the floor. The cage has two obvious advantages. First, if you really turn the car over, it will offer you a much greater level of protection. Second, it will tend to stiffen the body/chassis of the car, allowing for better and more predictable handling. On the other hand, the cage will weigh 25-40 pounds, take a tenth or two off your lap times, and make the cockpit of the car more inconvenient for general use. Further, your insurance company may have a very difficult time believing that this is still primarily a street car.

You might be imagining that you could put a removable cage in your car, so that you would have the advantage of it only on the track, and have your interior back the rest of the time. Unfortunately, it is very difficult to achieve the strength needed without welding the pieces together. You will either have a very expensive, complex and heavy structure, or you won't have the strength. In any case, the process of getting it in or out will never be exceptionally quick or easy.

4. Fire Extinguisher: You will need a fire extinguisher mounted so it is within your reach when you are strapped into the seat. The exact type and size varies by club. If you actually think you will ever need to use it, get the halon type. They are more expensive, but the dry-chemical types make an incredible mess that is very difficult to clean up.

5. Cooling system: Running your car at full throttle for 30 minutes at a time in the hot summer months will put heat stress on your engine. Once you have dealt with safety-related issues, keeping your engine safe and within proper temperatures is one of your top priorities. If you have a water- cooled car, you need to be sure that the cooling system is in top shape. Check belts and hoses regularly. If possible (within your budget and the rules under which you run) install a larger radiator, or see that more air gets to the radiator. Be sure that your coolant fluid is properly mixed and carry extra. Water alone is not adequate. Depending upon the rules, try to find a lower-temperature thermostat and a lower-temperature fan switch.

If you have an air-cooled car, be sure that nothing obstructs the natural flow of air to your engine. If it is allowed and needed, modify the car so more air flows over the engine.

6. Oil Cooling and System Integrity: It should be obvious that you need to use top-quality oil and filters. You cannot change the oil too often to suit a motor, especially if the motor runs hot. Oil breaks down with time and temperature. As oil breaks down, it no longer lubricates in the same way.

If the rules permit, install as large an external engine oil cooler as you can
reasonably fit onto your car. Such a system needs a thermostatic or pressure
relief system to avoid excess pressure when the oil
is cold. Also, the lines should be of extremely | *Do **not** oil the track* |
high quality and expertly installed. Aeroquip or
similar aircraft/racing quality lines and fittings are essential. Do not use push-on-
then-clamp fittings. You should also have both an oil temperature gauge and an
oil pressure gauge. Try to keep the oil temperature below 240°F. You also
should have a LARGE low oil pressure warning light. It is difficult to watch all
the gauges all the time when you are trying to drive your car right to its limit on
an interesting course, and you want to know right now if you lose oil pressure.

You want to be very sure that your oil system is very robust and that nothing can
come loose or break. It is not uncommon, at a time trial, to have a car develop
some sort of mechanical problem and spill oil on the track. This is often the
result of bad design or
sloppy maintenance of the | *Keep the oil system in top-notch shape* |
oil cooling system. The
effect on the event is that everything stops while crews of people with grease
sweep go out to get the track clean enough to be safe to drive on. However, the
effect right at the moment the oil begins spilling is to create a very major hazard
for the other cars on the track, particularly the ones right behind the car with the
problem. Depending on what breaks, you may even be spilling oil directly in
front of your own tires, which will nearly insure you a quick trip into the weeds,
or whatever lies beyond the edge of the track. You should be sure that your oil
system is in top shape so you don't create such hazards for other drivers or
become The Driver Who Oiled The Track Once More And Must Not Be
Allowed To Drive With Us Ever Again.

7. Transmission coolers: For the same reasons that you need maximum cooling
for your engine oil, you should consider increasing the capacity of any cooling
system for your transmission fluid. Such cooling is rather standard for automatic
transmissions. It is usually a relatively straightforward task to mount an
auxiliary oil radiator and re-plumb the car to use it instead of the one that came
with car. Be sure that you are using a more effective radiator than the one you
had.

8. Brakes: Brakes are always important, but rarely as important as when your
car is on a road track. You are trying to calculate braking points to the nearest
couple of feet, and you are really counting on the brakes to slow you down when
you need them. Pushing down on the brake pedal and finding that nothing
happens may have a very bad effect on your disposition, physical health and car's
sheet metal. There is simply no room for error with the brake system. Your
brakes have to be in top shape, and better than required for normal street use.

The function of brakes is to turn kinetic energy (your forward motion) into heat. This results in your having less forward motion and hot brakes. The brakes are designed to dissipate the heat into the air through which you are traveling. Many of the brake systems on cars that end up on the time trial track were not completely designed for the heavy use to which you will put them. In some cars you will notice that, during a practice session, the brake pedal becomes softer (more compressible), the point at which the pedal engages the brakes drops lower and lower toward the floorboard of the car, and the brakes work less well even when you push on them very hard. If your car doesn't do any of this, then you should say a few thankful words to whatever God you pray to, but read on so you are ready to cope with brake problems if they arise.

> *Brakes will tend to go away during a practice session*

Some drivers always double-pump the brakes. They give the pedal a quick push and release it before pushing on it for real. This comes from one too many experiences of pressing on the brake pedal and finding very little pedal there. If your brakes fade, this is one way to keep safe while you get back to the pits. Brakes in good working order shouldn't require this. Such a technique also requires you to lift your foot from the throttle earlier than otherwise necessary.

If you want to know a lot about brake systems, get your hands on a copy of Fred Puhn's book on brakes, listed in the bibliography.

8a. Brake Cooling: Because most of the problems with brakes are related to their being excessively hot, cooling the brakes is a very effective technique. This may or may not be permitted by the rules applicable to your class of car. For most cars, you should add as much brake cooling as your rules allow. Find a way to scoop air at the front of the car and force feed it onto the disk or into the drum of the front brakes. It is the front brakes that are doing most of the work, so concentrate on them first.

You may be able to find aftermarket scoops that sit below the front axle and that force air through a large hose directly onto the disk. Also, don't overlook the advantage of vented wheels in helping air flow over the brakes.

In most time trial practice sessions, drivers get a 'cool down' lap after the checkered flag. It is a good practice to use this lap to ease back on the motor and to let the brakes cool off. You do this by slowing down and trying to stay off the brakes. Even if you have done a proper cool down lap,

> *Use the checkered flag lap to cool down your engine and brakes*

your brake fluid will likely get hotter after you park the car in the pits. It may boil. If it does, you will find your pedal very soft when you go out for the next practice session. If this happens to you, you may need to bleed the brakes between each practice session.

8b. Brake Fluid: Brake fluid comes in several types. The type you want is one that has a high boiling point (over 550°F). If you manage to get some of the brake fluid boiling you will now have brake gas, rather than brake fluid, and the pedal will feel very spongy. You will also have a very difficult time stopping the car. Be careful of silicone-based brake fluid. While it does have a very high boiling point (about 750°F), it becomes compressible when hot and is not appropriate for a track car. The compressibility results in a soft feel to the brake pedal. There are good brake fluids available at automotive competition shops.

8c. Bleeding the Brakes: Part of the problem with the brakes becoming soft and spongy is not the fluid itself, but moisture that condenses into the brake fluid. At less than 212°F or so, the moisture is liquid and of no real concern. Once the braking system begins to get hot, the moisture present in the brake fluid right at the hottest places (nearest the pads or shoes) will vaporize, giving you gas in your brake system again and creating a soft brake pedal.

The method for removing accumulated gas in the system is to bleed the brakes. This is done by holding down the brake pedal and briefly opening a valve at the brake cylinder or caliper. The valve is positioned at the top of the area that contains the brake fluid, and any gases will be at the top. The

> *When brakes get soft and mushy, you need to bleed them*

valve is closed again before the brakes are released. A tube is placed over the output spout of the valve to keep air from being sucked back into the brake system. You can watch the fluid being expelled and see if there are any bubbles. If there are, your brakes should feel better next time you go out onto the track. If not, then accumulated gasses were not the problem, or you didn't get them out.

Over time, more and more moisture dissolves into the brake fluid. For this reason it is a good policy to change the brake fluid completely about once every year. The procedure is about the same as bleeding the brakes of accumulated gasses, except in two respects. First, when you begin, let the brake fluid in the master cylinder get low (but not so low as to introduce air into the system), then fill it up with new fluid. This way you will have the old fluid in the brake lines and mostly new fluid in the master cylinder. Now, as you continue to purge the system, the old fluid will be pushed through the lines and out into your container at each slave cylinder. The other difference is that you will have to pump much more fluid through the system to purge the old fluid.

When bleeding the brakes, be sure that you keep the master cylinder full of fluid so you do not introduce air into the system. Start with the wheel that is the furthest away from the master cylinder, and work your way around the car until you are at the wheel that is the closest to the master cylinder. One expert mechanic and chassis tuner, Dwight Mitchell, has found better success by starting with the wheel <u>closest</u> to the master cylinder, then working farther away. This will be effective if you are pumping a large amount of brake fluid out of the car. His theory is there may be some vapor trapped near the master cylinder, and that you are better off pushing this vapor the short distance to the nearest wheel, rather than leaving it trapped in the line between the master cylinder and the furthest wheel. Some disk brakes have two places to bleed the brakes on one caliper assembly. Be sure to bleed them both. Finally, brake fluid is hard on people and paint. Don't slop any around, and be sure to wash your hands well when you are done.

<u>8d. Brake Pads</u>: You may find that there are different brands of brake pads or shoes available for you car. Choose carefully, after listening to the people who are running a similar type of car. Dustless pads are often hard on the rotors and poor at stopping the car. Competition pads may require substantial heating before they begin to work effectively. These pads can be excellent for time trialing, but are a poor choice for a car that must autocross and time trial, as they will not heat sufficiently during an autocross run. They also may be dangerous for street use. It may take some trial and error to find the pads that you like the best. Don't get discouraged; once you find the ones that work, and know that you can count on the brakes to do a great job, life on the track gets very sweet.

After you have changed brake pads, it may take a pump or two on the brake pedal to get all the fluid where it belongs. The first pump may feel like you have no brakes at all. Just don't move the car until you have pumped the brakes a couple of times to assure yourself that everything is in order.

<u>8e. Brake Modifications</u>: In addition to adding cooling to the brakes, you may be able, under the rules for your class, to drill or slot the brake rotors or make other changes. Drilling seems less effective than slotting, but both approaches allow the gases created at the brake pad during braking to escape. If the gases don't escape, they form a vapor barrier between your brake pads and the rotor.

<u>9. Car Numbers</u>: Most time trials require that you have large numbers on two or four sides of your car. These make it convenient for the officials and turnworkers to talk about you, and they provide a 'name' for your car for scoring purposes. You may also be required to display the number or letter of the class in which you are competing, so your competitors can see who else is in their

class. These competitors may wish to meet you, to know who they are running against and they may wish to see if there is anything unusual about your car. The numbers will have to contrast with the color of your car. The required height and thickness of the numbers will be spelled out in the rulebook.

In some clubs you may be able to secure a permanent number to use during the entire season or, perhaps, as long as you continue to compete with the club. If you have a car that is dedicated to track use, or if you like running around on the street with numbers on your car, you may wish to paint them on. This presumes, of course, that the same numbers will suffice for all the events you run in the car. On the other hand, if you have a car that you want to keep nice, and you believe that running around on the street with 10" numbers may attract a lot of unwelcome attention, then you need a way to put numbers on your car temporarily.

Temporary numbers can be fashioned from colored duct tape, called racing tape and available from automotive competition stores. Be sure that the paint underneath is freshly waxed to avoid the possibility that the excellent adhesive on this tape will pull paint up when the

> *Car numbers made of racing tape are ugly, time-consuming or both*

numbers are removed. This approach is usually either time consuming or ugly; sometimes it is both.

A better approach is to purchase some sheet magnetic material from a local sign company or graphics shop. This can be cut to the shape you need and placed on the car when you are time trialing. When you are not time trialing the numbers can be stuck to the inside of any convenient flat surface, such as the underside of the trunk lid. When you cut the material, cut it at an

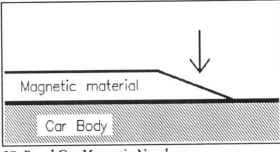

37 Bevel Cut Magnetic Numbers

angle. This makes it less likely that air will get underneath and peel the number off when you are going very fast.

The background of your letters can be the white top surface of the magnetic material, or you can apply contact paper in the color of your choice. If you wish to paint the magnetic material the color of your car, which makes for a very pretty effect, you will need to peel off the white top layer, then clean off the glue residue with lacquer thinner. It will then take paint quite nicely.

The letters themselves can be hand cut from contact paper. You can also buy them from racing supply shops, in a limited range of colors and sizes. Many modern graphics shops have a computer-based system that will cut numbers and letters from sticky-backed decal material in a wide variety of colors, sizes and typestyles. You may prefer to make each letter separately of magnetic material. This allows you some flexibility if you need to renumber your car, but you will have to tape them down every time, as the air rushing past your car will peel off the smaller numbers. Be sure to clean the surface before mounting the magnetics. This will give you better adhesion and prevent the process of mounting and removing the magnetics from scratching your paint.

10. Taping the Lights: You will be required to put tape over your headlights. This will mean that there is less glass flying around the air and left on the course should you have an 'incident' on course. To protect your car you might also want to tape up any other lights or turn signals in front. Some people tape the plastic rear turn signals; why they do this is not clear. Do not tape over the brake lights.

11. Car Bra: You will be closely following cars whose tires are picking up the grit on the track surface and throwing it at the front of your car. Cars with race tires are the worst in this regard, but all tires will pick up some of the grit. If you have a nice paint job, you may wish to have a bra on the car when you are on the track. Get one that fits tightly. Be careful not to leave the car sitting in the hot sun with the bra on but no car cover. Black bras pick up and radiate a great deal of heat, and can damage the paint of your car much more than a few chips from the cars in front of you. Be sure that the bra does not flap against the paint when you are moving. If it does, it will certainly damage the paint.

As an alternative to a bra, you can use helicopter tape on the front of the car. This is a soft, clear tape that comes in wide (and expensive!) rolls. It is used to protect helicopter rotors from chipping. Use it only on paint that is in good shape, not tending to peel off the car and not already badly chipped. The tape will peel up with effort, or you can use a hair dryer to heat the tape, at which point it will peel off easily.

12. Video Camera: Many people buy a photographic tripod head and mount it in the car, normally on some part of the rollbar. They can then mount a video camera in the car and take video movies as they drive around the track. There are both fun and practical reasons for this. The fun part is having a chance later to sit back and observe your driving on the track, and share the movies with your kids or friends. Of course, after a couple of hundred video laps around your

favorite course, you may find that friends drop by less often and your kids won't go near the television even for MTV.

On the practical side, you can spend non-track time doing a critique of your performance. You can also time yourself around various portions of the track to see what is your best time on any section. If you have been trying slightly different lines, this can be very useful. Either you will find out that one approach is clearly superior to another, or that it doesn't make any difference and you should just take the approach with which you are most comfortable.

> *The movies will get you into the groove*

Another good use for the movies is simply to spend time watching, an evening or two before going to a time trial. This is probably most worthwhile during your first few years of time trialing. While the movies do show the speed and the line, they do not seem to communicate the sense of lateral acceleration (being pushed sideways in the car and on the track). The movies also do not properly capture the subtle terror of drifting slightly sideways at speeds above 100 mph. Nevertheless, watching the movies will get you back into the mood of high-speed driving, and somewhat reduce those first-session jitters that are common for people new to the sport.

Video is more difficult to use with any precision for autocrossers. It normally cannot help study the track, as the track is different each day. It also doesn't 'see' the course quite as well as the driver, so it becomes difficult to see exactly where you are on the course, relative to the pylons. If you can find precise reference points, it can help two drivers of the same car compare their performance through specific sections of the course, giving each driver some clues as to where improvement may be available.

If you decide to get a camera, get one that is very small and compact. It will be subjected to strong forces as you brake and turn. A large camera is more difficult to mount strongly enough. There may also simply not be enough room for a large video camera. If possible, borrow or rent the model you want. Some models simply shut themselves off as the car gets bumped around.

13. Ear Plugs: Excessive noise is tiring and stressful to human beings. On the track, you will be confronted with a great deal of engine and wind and tire noise. Wearing ear plugs will help you stay more relaxed and less tired. You will also better concentrate on your driving. The best are the little foam cylinders. Whichever you get, be sure you can wear them with your helmet on. Don't worry about not being able to hear enough. All the tire, motor and transmission sounds that you are used to will be there, just at a more subtle volume. To help you remember to use them, attach the case to your helmet bag or your helmet.

J. Preparing Yourself

Slowly and methodically he unpacks the car. Out comes the ice chest, warm jacket, folding chair, spare tire, 5-gallon gas can, small toolbox, 1-gallon milk container full of water, air pump, jumper cables, racing-quality air pressure gauge, whisk broom, scissor jack and handle, thin tarp, torque wrench, each placed in a carefully learned pattern so things needed during the day will be easily at hand while the rest will be carefully covered with the tarp. Who would have thought that an Alfa-Romeo would even hold all this? And what had been the nearly unobserved process that led here from the time two years ago when he hadn't even known what some of these things were?

This chapter is devoted to the tools and supplies you will need to take care of you and your car at an event.

1. Have a Checklist: Many of the items in this chapter are not important until you don't have them. Then they become critical. The easiest solution is to have a personal checklist that you can review when you are preparing for an event. The capitalized words in this chapter will give you some ideas for your checklist. Don't be alarmed at the length of the list of things you might take to an event; for now, simply evaluate each item to see if you think you need it. After a few events, you will be able to decide what you really need.

2. Where and When: If the event requires pre-entry, be sure to get it in on time. Once you know the date of the event you are going to enter, be sure you know the exact LOCATION. Organizers often find autocross sites difficult to secure, and some of the sites may be a bit off the beaten path. It is always a good idea to have the phone number of someone who is not going to the event but who knows how to get there, in case you get completely lost. You need to know the TIME that you will run (and work), if the event is divided into run groups. Plan your schedule so you arrive with time to spare.

If the event is very far away you may need to make motel RESERVATIONS or take a van, camper or motorhome. If you are staying in your own vehicle, you will need to know where you can park it. If you are selecting hotel/motel

accommodations, try to find a place where your car will be relatively safe. Some
hotels provide security during the nighttime hours, a real plus if you have a
valuable car in good shape.

3. Helmets: Some clubs provide loaner autocross helmets for people who do not
bring their own, but, if you get very involved in solo racing you will want a good
HELMET that fits well. The helmet will need a Snell sticker. This sticker has a
date that indicates roughly when it was built. Most clubs require that the sticker
be relatively current. When your helmet no longer meets your club's
requirements you must buy a new one. Most clubs require a sticker that is less
than 10 years old.

Your helmet should fit properly. If it is too loose, it will not turn promptly
when your head does, and it will not offer optimal protection. If it is too tight,
you risk constricting blood flow to your brain. You probably won't pass out
from a tight helmet, but you may get a headache and you will find it more
difficult to concentrate on your driving. People who have never used a helmet
when driving a car or a motorcycle often find it distracting. Students not
accustomed to a helmet may wish to consider spending some time wearing one
around the house. One new autocrosser spent a couple of evenings watching TV
with a helmet on, with the goal of getting used to the sensation of wearing a
helmet by the time he got to the autocross school.

4. Other Clothing: You are planning to spend a day or two out in the elements.
Clothing should be comfortable rather than stylish, if a choice must be made.
SHOES should be comfortable recreation shoes with a good soft sole, as you will
be spending much of the day walking on pavement. Ideally, the shoes are light,
to make it easier to move your feet around while driving, and have soles thin
enough to give you some feel from the pedal. Sandals or thongs do not fit
securely enough to be safe. If you prefer to drive with GLOVES, they should be
thin, to give you the best possible feel for the steering wheel and gearshift.

Summer racing can make for a very hot day. In addition to whatever local
temperature you have, the asphalt surface will collect and radiate the heat. You
may want SHORTS and a T-SHIRT. You may want to consider taking a HAT, a
LONG-SLEEVE SHIRT and SUNTAN LOTION if the sun will be very intense.
Some people bring a large UMBRELLA to provide extra shade. There are tables
with umbrellas that fold down very compactly into a suitcase shape and provide a
nice family headquarters.

If the weather is cold, you will need a WARM JACKET and possibly a WARM
HAT. If there is a chance of rain, you will want a suitable RAIN HAT and
RAIN JACKET. Some events, including most time trials, will be cancelled due

to rain, but some autocrosses may run. Racing in the rain is actually a lot of fun, though quite different from normal competitive driving. Speeds are much slower and the car is usually very loose (sliding) at all times. If you do run in the rain, you will want some GALOSHES and TOWELS.

5. Tools & Car Supplies: Though there will usually be people who will loan you a small required tool in an emergency, it is good to carry whatever TOOLS you think you might need. This can range from a kit as simple as screwdrivers, pliers and a wrench set for the driver who just wants to be prepared to handle small problems, to a

> *Carry whatever tools you think you might need*

full tool box and a variety of parts and supplies. Tools include PAPER TOWELS, HAND CLEANER, and WINDSHIELD CLEANER. Car supplies include OIL, COOLANT, FUSES, FAN BELTS and the like. If you subscribe to the ritual of changing tires at the track, be sure to load your RACING TIRES, FLOOR JACK, JACK STANDS and TORQUE WRENCH. If you may need to bleed brakes, you will need BRAKE FLUID, a TUBE and a BRAKE FLUID BOTTLE for expelled brake fluid.

6. Air Pressure Stuff: You should have a good TIRE GAUGE. However, the tire gauge will not do you a lot of good if you don't have any way to inflate the tires. To add air to tires you need either a small PORTABLE AIR COMPRESSOR (available at automotive stores) that will run off your cigarette lighter socket, or an AIR BOTTLE that you can fill at a service station. Neither item is very expensive. The air bottle takes more room, but it works faster when you need it. The air bottle has only a limited amount of air. The compressor has the advantage of providing (slowly) as much air as you need.

You can, of course, just stop by a service station and get more air than you will need, and bleed out the excess at the track. However, if you over-bleed, or find that you have a slow leak, you won't be able to correct it. If you make a practice of checking tire rollover, you should have a bottle of WHITE SHOE POLISH.

7. Other Things: Take a small FOLDING CHAIR. There will be times when you are neither running nor working, and it is more relaxing to sit in the chair than to have to stand all day. Bring a STOPWATCH. If you are a member of a car club and have a club NAME BADGE, be sure to take it and wear it. It helps people to learn your name. Also, take along a pad of PAPER and a PEN, so you can make notes and sketch the course. If you have a set of CAR NUMBERS, bring it. If you are being sponsored, bring your SPONSOR'S DECALS to put on the car. It is also nice to have a TARP to cover all the stuff that comes out of your car at an event; this will reduce the chance that things might decide to walk

off. Whether or not there is any risk of theft really depends on the group of people who are there. In most cases your stuff is very safe.

8. Living Supplies: Life doesn't stop at an event, so you have to take some basic supplies with you. Obviously, you should have enough MONEY to cover anything you will need to buy. You will need food and beverage. At some events you can expect to have a concession stand or a catering truck, but such is not always the case. It is always a good idea to bring a COOLER with some WATER, LUNCH, SNACKS and SOFT DRINKS. Alcoholic beverages are strictly

| *Bring an ice chest* |

prohibited to entrants and spectators at all events until they are over. If, at the end of the day, you just can't wait until everyone gets to pizza and beer, you may take along some BEER or WINE in the cooler as well. Just don't pop that top until the the last car has run.

9. Rest: Plan the night before an event so you can get an adequate amount of REST. If you care about your lap times, you will not be partying and drinking late into the night.

K. Working an Autocross Course

The drivers still willing to admit that they have a little to learn are easy to find. They are in the infield of the course <u>before</u> they run, watching carefully how the course is being driven by the best drivers. When they can see the back of the car they are looking carefully at the brake lights, determining where the driver is applying the brakes, and for how long. Sometimes they find that a turn that looked, when walking the course, like it would require brakes is being handled with just a brief lift of the throttle. They listen to the engine very carefully, trying to tell when the throttle is being feathered and when the engine is being asked to give everything it can. And they watch the exact lines being driven. All of this is compared to the lap times heard on the PA, so they have a sense of what techniques are actually producing the lowest times.

It takes a lot of work to run an autocross; it is all for a noble cause, but work nonetheless. This work is provided by the competitors when they are not driving. Everyone must work. The safety and fun of the event depends upon the competitors themselves, when they are working, doing their job in a safe, diligent and competent manner. This chapter is to get you ready to do the various jobs that have to be done. The worker jobs associated with time trialing are beyond the scope of this book. Such events take a great deal more effort to organize and run than a parking-lot autocross, and the worker jobs are often more complex. Most of the organizers of such events have very solid programs in place for training the workers at the various positions to an appropriate level.

1. Signing up for Work: At most autocrosses you sign up for work when you register. Usually, there is a large plastic board and a grease pen or marker. Simply put your name into a slot by a position for which you are qualified. Find out how many slots each entrant is supposed to fill in and fill in that many with your name. In some cases there are specific times for working, in other cases there are two or more run groups and your group works while another group runs. The beginning autocrosser should always try to spend some time as a courseworker, as this is an excellent way to observe

Beginning autocrossers should spend much time as courseworkers

the techniques being used by other drivers. Over time, you should try to learn most of the jobs so you will be able to help out where needed.

2. Be At Your Job Early: Course time is usually scarce. Sites are hard to find, and the course may have to be shut down at a certain time or by dark. Time spent not running any cars while waiting for people to get to their work stations is wasted time and is never recovered. The solution is this: when you have completed all the runs you are going to get before you have to work, put your car wherever it needs to be while you work and go relieve the person who has been

38 Signing up to work

working your job. The extra five minutes of work should not be life-threatening to you, and you will ultimately get MORE RUNS.

3. Don't Be Afraid to Ask for Help: Everyone has a first time at each job they ever do. Some jobs are difficult to learn from just one sitting (or standing, as the case may be). Some jobs may not be completely remembered if the last time you did the job was three months ago. People will be delighted that you want to do it right, and will be

> *Time spent not running cars is wasted and is NEVER RECOVERED*

tickled to help you learn. So, if you are unsure about how to do the job, ask any of the people around. If they don't know, they will find someone who does.

4. Flagperson: The flagperson is in charge of the course and determines when people enter the course and leave it. The flagperson stands near start/finish, out of the way of directions in which cars may spin or slide should they err on the side of exuberance coming through the turn just before start/finish. If it is start-here-finish-there course, the flagperson stands near the start area and will need only green and red flags. The flagperson is responsible for insuring that there are enough courseworkers. Four or five courseworkers are usually enough.

For closed courses, three flags are normally used: green, red and checkered. The checkered flag indicates to the drivers that they are finished and should exit the course. The red flag is used only when an emergency has developed or is about to develop and indicates that the driver must stop the car immediately and await further instructions from the flagperson or a courseworker. Courseworkers are expected to get their red flags waving immediately if they see the flagperson waving a red flag. The green flag is used to tell the driver to proceed onto the course, or, when the car is already on course, to continue driving.

When only one car is on course at a time (this is called 'non-overlap') the sequence for the flagperson is as follows:

• Using a furled green flag, point at the next car to come out. This tells the driver to be ready to move out very soon. The driver should acknowledge your signal.

• To flag the driver onto the course, wave the open green flag back and forth, or above your head, or swing it furled in a circle over your head. Use any variation that seems to work, but don't get too cute, lest the drivers become confused about what you are trying to signal.

• As soon as the car begins to enter the course, immediately stop waving the flag, hold it open and visible to the driver and show, with fingers on the hand not holding the flag, the number of laps the driver is to drive.

• Each time (except the last time) that the car comes by start/finish, hold out a stationary green

39 Flagman shows 2 laps

flag and indicate by number of fingers the number of laps remaining in the run. Be sure not to obstruct the driver's vision of the turn just beyond start/finish.

• On some occasions the timer may fail to start when the car enters the course, or, if a practice lap is being given, when the car completes the first lap. In some clubs you are supposed to red-flag the car immediately. In less formal environments, you can try to give the car an extra lap. The driver, of course, doesn't know that the clock has not started. Their next time around, shake the green flag at them VERY AGGRESSIVELY. Try to get the driver to see that the number of fingers being held up is one more than they might expect.

• Drivers who do not see the signal for extra laps and pull off the course at the end of the normal number of laps, will be given a re-run. However, this takes extra time. It is important that the driver watch the flagperson and follow the signals given.

• When the driver is coming by start finish for the last time, wave the checkered flag so the driver knows the run is complete and to exit the course.

● Bring the next car onto the course

When more than one car is on the course at the same time, for a brief time, known as 'overlap', the flagperson's job becomes a little more complex. After the first car comes onto the course, all subsequent cars will be flagged on when the car on the course is completing its last lap.

Use a key point on the course to gauge when to flag the next car on. Choose this point very carefully. It should be after any cross-overs, so the cars don't run the risk of meeting at the intersection. Ideally, it should also be after any turns on which the drivers seem to spin often. On the other hand, it cannot be too late in the lap, or the entering car will present a hazard to the car that is finishing its run.

Also note that it is IMPERATIVE that the entering car be paying very close attention to the flagperson. If the entering driver does not immediately notice being flagged onto the course, then, all of a sudden, checks into reality and charges out onto the course, that driver may end up directly in the path of the first car.

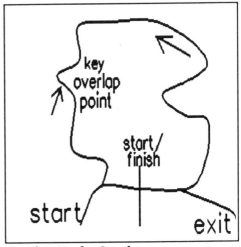

40 Flagging for Overlap

As an example, the flagging sequence for overlap, if the event is being run as one practice lap and two timed laps would be

[S/F = start/finish]
flag car 1 onto the course - as it passes S/F, show 3 fingers for 3 laps
car 1 passes S/F again, starts clock - show two fingers
car 1 passes S/F again - show one finger (index)
point furled flag at next car
when car 1 gets to the key point on course - flag car 2 onto the course

show car 2 standing green flag and three fingers
car 1 comes by S/F last time - wave checkered flag, car leaves course
    [make SURE the car actually leaves the course]
car 2 comes by start/finish, starts clock - show two fingers
car 2 comes by start/finish again - show one finger (index)
etc., etc., etc.

The flagperson needs to pay constant attention to the car(s) on course and ready to enter the course, and be ready to call for a red flag if necessary. If in doubt, take the safest course you have available. With experience you will become accurate and confident about what actions you should take. Better to be safe and have a few people grumbling than to risk bent sheet metal or personal injury. If you're not <u>sure</u> that you can safely let a car onto the course, don't.

While it seems easy enough to keep track of which lap a car is on while on the course, it is not uncommon for you suddenly to realize that you

> *Better to be safe and have a few people grumbling than risk bending sheet metal or injuring someone*

have NO IDEA how many laps remain for the car now on course. This will usually happen during the middle of a work session when the cars have settled down to a solid routine and you begin to think about other things.

If you have any honor at all, this is a personally serious situation. If the car is flagged off the course too soon, the driver will have to be given a re-run. The driver will probably be happy for the extra practice, but fierce competitors in the driver's same car class will be less than completely tickled. On the other hand, an extra lap may allow the current run to count, but will still provide extra practice and will take time away from other drivers. In either case you appear to be incompetent. Additionally, if the driver waiting on the starting gate is counting the laps, you may find that car responding to unintentional flag movements and coming out onto the course a lap earlier than you had planned. This would be a rare

41 Number of Laps

sequence of events, but it must be avoided. If the second car is much slower or faster, and if you have a crossover on the course, you end up with cars much too close to each other.

Usually, you can call out to the timing table and people will tell you where you are in the sequence, but it is better to prevent the problem in the first place. The prevention is a simple trick of how you hold the green flag. The trick is to determine how many fingers you will show the driver the next time the car comes around, then wrap that number of fingers around the loose end of the flag. Then, when you realize that you have NO IDEA how many laps remain, you can just look down at the fingers and know exactly what is going on.

The final note on flagging concerns safety. Spins are caused by an oversteering condition of some sort. Depending on what actions the driver takes during the spin, cars often end up on the <u>inside</u> of the turn they failed to negotiate. The inside of the turn just before start/finish is about where you will be standing. This is not a severe danger, unless you are not paying attention. Autocross courses are normally designed with a tight turn just before start/finish, so the car will be traveling relatively slowly. However, you should remain constantly aware that it may be necessary to move out sharply if someone blows the turn.

For start-here-finish-there courses the flagperson's job is a bit easier. You must keep an eye on the course, and not bring out another car if a car on course has spun out. You need to pick your 'next car' point, then bring a new car out each time the previous car reaches that point.

5. Timing (timer): The timing   **42 *Timing crew with self-appointed supervisor***
crew, usually two to four
people, has to work together. Several cars are in process at once, from the car which has just completed its run, waiting for a timing slip, to the car that just got to the starting gate, which needs its registration form to be found, ready for recording times.

5a. Running the Timer: The timing person who is running the automatic timing equipment must find out, from someone who knows, how the specific equipment operates. There are several different types of timers in use. The clock starts automatically when the car crosses start/finish. In some cases a split-time is displayed automatically when the car comes by start/finish a second time; the internal clock will keep running. In other cases two clocks are linked together, the first

43 *Running the Timer*

is used for the split time, and the second is used for the overall time. With the fully automatic timers all the timer need do is push a reset button just before the car on course starts its first timed lap. In other cases the timer must frequently switch one or both switches, and reset everything before the next car starts its timed lap. The person running the timer must be sure that the people recording the time on entry forms have a chance to see the time accurately before resetting the clock.

If there is a serious automatic timer malfunction that cannot be corrected at the course, the cars must be timed by hand. The best approach involves using three people to time, each person using a hand stopwatch. Times may be averaged or the middle time may be used. Using the middle time is simpler and there are some reasonable statistical arguments that it is preferable to an average.

5b. Timing (entry form): The person recording times on the entry form must note in advance the next car that is coming onto the course. This is done either by looking over at the grid person running the number board and reading the number displayed, or by listening on the headset to the worker located where the next car awaits being flagged onto the course. The form is pulled from wherever it is filed, then left open on the table where the announcer can

44 Timing Lights

read the name and other information and announce who is running next. The timing person writing on the logsheet also needs to see the form. The split time, if any, and the final time are recorded on the form as soon as available from the automatic timer. Pylon penalties, if any, are also noted and an official time computed by adding the pylon penalty to the total time. The normal pylon penalty is one second per pylon added to the scratch time, but some clubs add two seconds per pylon. The card is then re-filed for use next time the driver drives.

It is also the responsibility of this worker to note if the driver has already completed the number of runs allotted by this point in the event. If so, the flagperson should be informed not to allow the car to enter the course. Do this gently, as there is a chance of error; tension will likely arise when drivers are prevented from taking a run to which they are entitled.

45 Handling Log Sheets

5c. Timing (logsheet): The worker recording times on the logsheet reads the times from the automatic timer and fills out the form being used. Some of the information will be on the entry form. Typical information is the car number, the driver's name, the car classification, the split time, and the final time. Pylon penalties, if any, are also noted. These forms will be used by the posting person.

<u>5d. Timing Slip Runner:</u> This is a fairly light-duty job. It involves taking the completed timing slip from the timing people and handing it to the driver who has just come off the course. Keep in mind that you are the first person the driver talks to after the run. The time you are handing out may not be what the driver needed or wanted, so some of the drivers may seem pretty grumpy.

46 *Some autocrossers start young. This one hands out timing slips*

<u>5e. Posting:</u> The posting person takes the logsheet of official times and enters them onto result sheets posted somewhere near the timing area, usually organized by the cars' classifications. The data normally entered is simply the total time, with some indication of pylon penalties, if any. The board may also be used to post year-to-date standings in the series.

<u>6. Announcer:</u> The announcer typically stands near the timing area where the entry forms are easily visible and the driver's name can be read. The name of the driver, the class of the car and all split times and final times should be announced in a clear voice. The region or home town of the driver may be announced, along with a description of the car and any other information about the car or the driver the announcer may have and wish to share. A certain amount of kidding and joshing (and that 'certain amount' is sometimes large indeed) is expected, but the announcer should take care that comments are not insulting or demeaning unless the friendly intent is unmistakable. Comments about the beauty of the car (or lack of same) may be made.

47 *Posting Times*

Comments should also be made about the car on the course, how well it is being driven, etc. Spins, off-course excursions and the knocking over of pylons should all

> *Comments should not be insulting or demeaning unless the friendly intent is unmistakable*

be mentioned. From the entry form, which includes results of runs earlier in the day, the announcer can also see whether the driver has a better split or final time than previous efforts, and this can be mentioned.

If you are on top of the situation, see if the driver is doing better or worse than other people driving the same car. Or, see if you can figure out how the driver now places in class. You can't do all this the first time you announce, but after you get more familiar with the people and the classes, you will be better able to keep track of the key battles.

At events where workers do not communicate with headphones, the announcer plays an even more important role, sharing with the flagperson immediate control over the event. If a car needs to be red-flagged, the announcer should point this out loudly to any course workers who may be insufficiently attentive.

48 *Announcing*

7. Grid: The people working the grid are responsible for determining and enforcing the order in which cars make their runs. The job normally includes two people at the grid itself, and one person at the starting gate.

7a. Main Grid: This is often a two-person job, with one person running the main grid and the other being responsible for sequencing the second driver line, which may be a little ways away. In such cases the grid people must be in good and constant communication with each other, as there is just one sequence of cars onto the course and they cannot both send a car out at the same time.

For each run group (when more than one run group is used), there will be a grid open time (earliest time a car in that group can arrive on grid) and a grid close time (after which no additional cars are allowed on grid). As soon as the grid has closed, the grid person must collect the registration cards and take them to the timing people.

The normal procedure for sequencing cars onto the course is to run through a row of cars at a time, for as many rows **49** *Working Grid* as are necessary during the run group. For those of you into computer spreadsheets and matrix mathematics, yes, these rows should probably be called 'columns'. However, you will find them called 'rows' at most events, the same way you would refer to a row of corn.

In some autocross formats that will be the entire grid (all cars at the event). In other cases the cars will be running in groups, and only the cars in the current group will cycle at one time. The reason to set up the grid to run one row at a time is so only the drivers in the active row have to be constantly moving their cars up to the front of the row, getting ready to run. For this reason, do <u>not</u> cycle across the fronts of the rows, taking one car from each row.

It is the grid worker's responsibility to inform the announcer (via a very loud voice or a friend who is willing to act as runner) when it is time for the drivers of the next row to begin getting their cars ready. This is not to say that the drivers themselves shouldn't be paying close attention, because they should be. However, it is still up to the grid person to get the news onto the PA system.

Cars being driven by more than one driver should be brought to the second-driver line after the first person drives. The second driver line will normally be at one end of the grid or the other. After the last driver drives the car, it is returned to its original row to await the next run of the first driver of the car.

Sequencing the cars in the second driver line into the flow of cars onto the course can be tricky. The normal way to handle this is to alternate one car from the second driver line with one car from the current line on grid. The advantage of this approach is that all drivers can be told rather accurately how many cars it will be until it is their turn.

> *A good gridworker must be a good communicator*

However, when many cars have second drivers, or when cars are being driven by three or four drivers, this system can break down, with more and more cars piling up in the second driver line and the grid becoming increasingly chaotic. In such cases it may be necessary to give priority to the second driver line, letting each car there go as soon as the driver is ready. The moral justification for this approach is that the second driver in the car has already been held up and should be allowed to drive as soon as ready. Unfortunately, it is no longer possible to tell drivers in the regular line how many cars remain before they can run, and this may cause some resentment.

In all cases the grid person should keep the next few drivers aware of how many cars are slotted in front of them so the drivers can be ready to go when their turn comes around, yet not have to sit in a constant state of readiness thinking that they may be called on to move out on two-second's notice. This communication is one of the more important aspects of working grid, and can mean the difference between everyone having a pretty good time and situations getting somewhat tense. To be a good gridworker you will need to organize things well and communicate very effectively.

When grid space is limited, the grid person should also see that cars in the row that is currently being cycled onto the course move up in the line as soon as they are able. The typical problem lies not with the drivers about to run, for they are checking out the car, getting mentally ready, and are pretty aware of staying close to the action. Rather, when the first person in a row completes a run and drives around to the back of the row, there will still be several cars in the row, waiting to run. They may not have even moved yet. So, the just-returned driver will park the car and begin to unwind, maybe go over to timing to check how this run stacks up against the in-class competition, talk to friends about the run, get a soft drink from the cooler, whatever. In the next few minutes more cars from the row will leave to run, more cars will return, and here sits the first car in the row, about 8 car-lengths back from the front of grid. It is best, of course, if the drivers stay around until all the cars in the row are once again properly parked, but this does not always happen. It _is_ reasonable for the grid person to release the parking brake, shift the car into neutral and push it forward as needed. The grid person should never start the motor of the car.

Most clubs have specific rules about passengers. The grid workers have the primary responsibility for enforcing these rules. Some clubs do not allow passengers at all. In other cases, either the driver or the passenger

> *The gridworker must enforce the club's rules about passengers*

must be a qualified instructor. Some clubs allow passengers as long as they are registered to drive, or are at least 18 years old. At some events anyone can be a passenger.

7b. Laying out the Grid: In some cases, the people signed up to work grid during the first session will need to set up the grid area. When you do this, be sure that you leave room for rows that are long enough (about 10 cars long is typical) and wide enough that drivers can open their doors without banging into another car. You also need to be sure that you have enough rows. There will be one row for second drivers. For the most common event schedules, there will need to be enough rows to handle two run groups. If you aren't sure, someone should be able to estimate for you the reasonable maximum number of cars in a run group for this club. If you are running a single run group, then the grid will have to accommodate the total number of cars that are expected.

50 Number board

7c. Grid (starting gate): It is the responsibility of the grid person at the starting gate (who is often on the signup board as the third grid person), to inform timing of the number of the car that is awaiting its turn to come onto the course. In some cases this worker uses a radio headset. In other cases the number board person must use a large number board which has numbers that are flipped over to display the correct number. The board must be located in such a way that the people in the timing booth can see it without being obstructed by the cars that are waiting or by spectators.

8. Courseworker: Courseworker is one of the most important positions at an autocross, for the safety of the event depends more on alert courseworkers than on any other position. The worker at the right, while looking quite casual, is paying close attention to the cars on course. Working the course can be boring or exciting, depending upon how you approach it, but it is critical that it be competently done. The boring part may be just standing around, watching car after car circulate around the course, waiting for your turn to run. On the other hand, pylons that are knocked over must be reset immediately if not sooner, without getting in the way of the same or next car (the driver is NOT expecting to see running bodies in the middle of the course). Courseworkers should <u>never</u> endanger themselves by stepping in front of cars that are moving at speed.

51 Courseworker

Working the course provides an opportunity to watch closely the exact line and stylistic approach being taken by the various drivers, particularly the

> *Under <u>no</u> circumstances should courseworkers endanger themselves by stepping in front of a moving car*

fast drivers. This is especially valuable if you are only going to get a couple of runs at the course. By watching, you can see what similar cars can actually achieve in terms of turn speed and brake points.

The course worker is responsible for being generally aware of all cars on the course and acutely aware of the car when it is in the general area being worked. The courseworkers should disperse themselves evenly around the course, and not stand together in one group having a nice debate about tire pressures or the correct line for this course. Courseworkers need to stand well to the inside of the course, and not directly in the visual path of a car heading toward a turn. Therefore, do not position yourself directly at the end of a straightaway, nor too close to the outside edge of a turn. There are few things so distracting to a conscientious driver on course as having to worry about whether that *!#% courseworker is close enough to the course to constitute a true safety hazard, requiring the responsible driver to stop the car, explain the situation, then try to get a re-run.

The course worker should always carry a red flag with the pole and the loose corner held in one hand. Do <u>not</u> hold the flag loose, as the drivers are supposed to stop at the sight of an open red flag. The flag should NOT be rolled up. It takes too long to unroll it unless you have the presence of mind to

52 Courseworkers quickly setting up cones. Notice the cone in the air, thrown to the second worker to speed setup

Leave the red flag unrolled

grab the loose end and pull, while letting the handle of the flag rotate in your other hand. Such presence of mind is uncommon during emergencies, and needing to get a car stopped RIGHT NOW qualifies as an emergency. More than once I have seen a courseworker running across the infield of a course, shaking a rolled flag (which is really no more than a red stick) at a car, trying to get the car to stop. Do NOT roll up the flag.

Sometimes there are more course workers than red flags. There are usually at least six red flags. Those who do not have flags should set up and call out pylons as needed and keep a close eye on the events in their section.

All cars must be observed extremely carefully until they pass into someone else's area

The red flag is not often used, but when it is used it is critical that everyone respond optimally. A car may be red-flagged at the discretion of the flagperson, the announcer or the courseworker. When the announcer calls out "RED FLAAAAAAG," or the flagperson begins waving a red flag, or any course worker begins waving a red flag, it is the responsibility of <u>ALL</u> workers carrying red flags IMMEDIATELY to begin waving the flag in a way such as to be visible to all drivers on the course. The worker should run to a position near (but not ON!) the course while waving the red flag. The worker's first responsibility is not to get hit by the car. The second responsibility is to get the car to stop by any available means.

Course workers are also responsible for resetting pylons that are knocked over or knocked out of position, then informing the pylon counter or the flagperson of the number of pylons that were knocked over or knocked completely out of their box. Pylons that are moved, but still upright and still have some portion of their base within the marked box, need to be reset but are not counted against the driver. It is traditional to signal such pylons with a baseball 'safe' signal (arms extended to the side of the body, hands held palm-down, at about waist level). It is also important that the courseworker not count pylons knocked down on a practice lap.

To reset moved pylons, the courseworker must see which pylons are moved. To do this the worker needs to watch the pylons around and just behind EACH

53 *Pylons and Chalk Marks*

AND EVERY CAR that comes into his/her sector. All cars must be meticulously observed until they pass into someone else's area. One clue that some courseworker has failed to see a pylon get moved is repeated cries of "CONE, CONE, CONE, CONE" coming from the flagperson, the announcer, spectators or other workers.

9. Pylon Counter: The pylon counter is responsible for reporting to the timing people the number of pylons penalized on a given run. Sometimes this worker position is explicitly noted on the signup sheet, other times one of the people who have signed up for course work is expected to do the pylon counting. The pylon counter will either have a radio headset or there will be a few large signs with numbers painted on them (usually on both sides). The number '0' is displayed unless there were one or more pylons knocked down, in which case the number of penalty pylons is displayed. One of the boards, if boards are used, has a large 'X'. This signifies a Did Not Finish (DNF) and is displayed when the driver didn't complete the course per the rules in effect. Normal rules specify that drivers who get all four wheels off the

54 *Pylon Counter signaling one cone*

course must re-enter the course at the same spot they left it. Failure to do this normally counts as a DNF.

The Pylon counter needs to exercise special diligence that pylons knocked over by a driver on a practice lap are not counted against the car still on course that is just finishing its run. It is also important that pylons knocked over by the car just finishing its run not be counted against the practice or first lap of the car just coming onto the course, but the driver of that car is also responsible for seeing the down pylon and coming to a complete stop until the course worker corrects the conditions and sends the car back for a re-run. Such procedures are obviously not foolproof when it comes to pylons that are still standing but in the wrong place, as it is very hard for the driver to see the box marks around the pylon. The data about the number of pylons knocked over or out of the box (unfortunately, it isn't always just one at a time) will come from the courseworkers. This is another reason that it is very important for the course workers to watch carefully.

55 Pylon counter signals a DNF. Large smile shows it may have been a competitor in his class

10. Registration: The person doing registration will normally be in charge of greeting the entrant pleasantly, collecting money, assuring that the release form is signed, returning entry forms (which usually include a technical inspection form on the back), assuring that the entrant signs up for the required work slots and seeing that the entrant is aware of the various handouts that are often available. In some cases entrants will

> *Do NOT count pylons against the wrong car*

need to address an envelope to have event results mailed to their homes. There may be handouts or simply one posted copy of such things as the course map or the schedule for the event. The registration person should know the direction in which the course will be run and where tech is located, as these are the most typical questions on the minds of the entrants once they have registered.

11. Technical Inspection: The person doing technical inspection will have a checklist to follow. There are some judgement calls (how loose may the wheel bearings be, for example, or whether the tires are really worn past the specified limit), and these must be learned from people already competent in technical inspection. Technical inspection may happen on the grid or at an area reserved for technical inspection. When you are doing this job simply be sure that the car conforms to all of the checkoff items and then sign it off.

If you find a problem and are considering rejecting a car, be very diplomatic and gentle. Many of the people who attend car-oriented events will tend to react badly to any criticism of their vehicle. In most cases a problem can be corrected on

| *Be very gentle when rejecting a car* |

the spot. If you can guide the owner to someone likely to help solve the problem, then that will ease tensions as well.

12. Course Setup: If you arrive promptly in the morning, you may choose to help people set up the course. There are several ways you can help. Once the cones are set up, they will all need to be boxed. You 'box' cones by drawing a box around them, using small strips of construction drywall (plasterboard). Portions of the course will probably have a lot of gravel on them; this needs to be swept off to the side. In some areas of the country people routinely draw a chalk line at each edge of the course. An athletic field chalker is used to do this. It can't be done until the course is set up and the cones are in place, and yet the chalker can't be pushed along the edge with the cones in place. The best approach involves three people. One walks ahead, moving cones out of the way. The second pushes the chalker. The third person follows behind and scoots the cone back into position. All the cone movement can be done with feet only, avoiding the back strain of bending over constantly for 20 or 30 minutes.

L. Autocross Schools

The autocross instructor and student are both belted into the car, helmets on. As they are flagged onto the course the instructor says, "Remember, if I say 'gas' I want you to use all the throttle. If I say 'brake', it's probably too late already." By the third lap the student is beginning to trust the instructor, and is using the throttle and brakes much more aggressively. As the student enters the sweeper faster than on the previous run, he panics and lifts his foot entirely off the throttle. The car rapidly begins spinning, then comes to a stop amidst a litter of pylons. "Well," says the instructor, "let's review what happens when you lift in the middle of a fast turn."

1. What is an Autocross School?: In a certain sense, most club autocrosses are autocross schools, as instructors are normally available to anyone who asks. Some events that are promoted as schools are actually informal autocrosses where extra emphasis is placed on instruction. In these cases the morning is often reserved for students only, with the afternoon run times available to students, instructors and other autocrossers.

A two-day, weekend school normally involves using the first day for lecture (very little) and exercises designed to teach specific driving skills. For the exercises, the class will likely be broken into four to six run groups. Each group works on one exercise for *The class is broken into run groups* an hour or an hour and a half, or so, then all the groups rotate to the next exercise. Thus, the student will get a chance to work on all the exercises by the end of the day.

The instructor is normally in the car with the student whenever the exercises are being run. Two or three students may share one instructor. The instructor will move between cars as needed to be with each student for each try at the exercise. It is typical to rotate instructors so any given student will have three or four instructors during the weekend. This provides the student with a broad range of input.

The second day will be spent running an autocross course. The instructors may be allowed some time at the beginning of the day to run the course. This is both a reward for being at the school to instruct, and a chance to find out the best way to drive the course, so the students can be coached more expertly. Students normally ride with their instructors during this time. The rest of the day will be devoted to students driving the course with instructors riding as passengers.

2. How the Exercises Run: In a two-day school, the introductory portion will be the Saturday exercises. Each student will get several chances to run each exercise. Normally the student will take five or six laps around each exercise. It doesn't seem like much track time, with a typical cycle being 40 seconds of running and 10 minutes of waiting, but the track time is very intense, and you will be exhausted by the end of the day. The exercises covered in the rest of this chapter are a sampling of what you might find at an autocross school.

3. Skid Pad Exercise: This is the best exercise to do first. What you will learn will be to transfer weight to the front of the car (by lifting the throttle) or the back of the car (by pressing down on the throttle) and inducing oversteer and understeer, respectively. This exercise should be done first, as the process of using throttle to help steer the car is basic to all other aspects of controlling the car at the limit.

56 Skid Pad

You will normally take four to six revolutions around the skid pad each time out, then exit and get back onto the waiting grid. The first time out, just get the car up to the limits of traction, maintaining relatively steady throttle, until you begin to deal with the car starting to come loose. On the second and subsequent passes, get the car up to the limits of traction, then let off the throttle and experience the oversteer. Then apply strong throttle and experience the understeer. Work on this until you can control the car's direction with little use of the steering wheel and accurate use of the throttle. Be sure to run the skid pad in both directions.

57 Braking

4. Braking: This is a relatively simple exercise designed only for practicing braking points. The sides of the triangle are relatively long, so you will build up a little bit of speed. On a normal run you will take four laps or so, then return to grid. Work on maintaining full throttle until you have to brake, then using the brakes as hard as possible without locking up the tires. Many students have a tendency to brake too late, and are unable to get back on the throttle at the proper point. You should avoid this. Brake hard, but early enough so you are on the throttle when you need to be.

5. Slalom: The easiest way to set up a slalom exercise is the one shown in the diagram, a pair of standard 4- or 5-pylon slaloms, joined by two easy 180° sweepers. You will cycle through the course four times or so.

On an oversteering car, work on smooth transitions and a smooth, constant, (but determined) application of the throttle as the car rounds the cone. Be sure that throttle lifts (and braking, if needed) are performed while the car is heading straight (just passed one cone, but not yet turning for the next). If your car is understeering, counteract with throttle-lift as you turn.

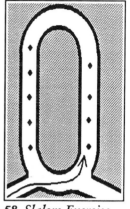

Notice that you must turn the car before the cone, to allow for the time the car takes to respond to steering input.

58 *Slalom Exercise*

6. Apexes: This course consists of a figure with a square bottom and a pointy top. Its purpose is twofold: first, to practice late apexes in standard turns, with most braking done in a straight line before beginning the turn (all braking, if you are fighting oversteer), throttle smoothly applied before turning the car into the corner, and continued application of throttle until completing the turn, all while properly selecting a late apex; second, the pointy turn is to help you learn to stay wide in the beginning of a turn when the proper apex is around the other side (the first apex pylon in this turn is a desperately early apex, which you need to learn to ignore, in favor of the pylon further around the turn).

You will cycle through the exercise area four times or so, then exit and return to the waiting line. Work on apex selection (especially the hidden apex on the pointy turn), braking before turning and beginning to get the throttle down before turning in. Also be sure you are entering the turn from the very outside of the turn, hitting the apex (within inches) and using the entire course width at the exit

59 *Apex Exercise*

of the turn. Note whether you have to lift after the apex. If so, this means that you turned in too soon.

Course room permitting, and after discussing it with your instructor, you may wish to use the square corners to go ahead and lift the throttle during the turn. While schools are NOT normally trying to teach the wrong way to drive, it might be useful to try to get that lifting-during-a-turn-that-gets-scary OUT of your system, and experience how the car feels during a spin. This should do the trick, by demonstrating to yourself the effect of lifting during the turn; that is, by proving to yourself the importance of getting the throttle down at the right point and keeping it down during the turn.

7. Oval: Some schools will use an oval with very short straight sections and even-radius sweeper turns. The objective here is to work on braking and apex selection. You may also be able to work on rotating the car near the end of the sweeper through a brief lift of the throttle.

60 Oval

You will take about four revolutions of the course then exit the course and return to the waiting grid. The course should be run in both directions before you are done with it. Work on proper braking technique and timing (no coasting, wait 'till brakes are needed then really use them), application of throttle before beginning the turn, and proper apex selection. If you are handling the basic exercise well, you may be able to come in a little hot, lift the throttle briefly at the right point (about 3/5ths of the way through the sweeper), then stand on the throttle to shoot the car down the straight. Do not try this without discussing it with your instructor.

8. Double Box: This exercise consists of two boxes connected together. It is an advanced exercise, good for practicing linking turns together. You will run the pattern three or four times, then exit and return to grid. Work on staying on your line, and slow down if you need to, to maintain the line.

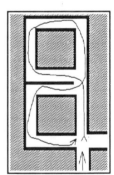

61 Double Box

9. Decreasing-Radius (figure 8): This is a figure 8 which conveniently contains two decreasing-radius turns, one to the left and the other to the right. It does not make any difference which way the course is run.

You will take about four cycles around the course, then exit and get back onto grid. Apply a modest amount of brakes if necessary, but work mostly on using throttle-off oversteer, induced by lifting the throttle somewhat, after starting the turn, to slow the car and continue turning the car in. Start slowly the first time out, then gradually move up to the limits of what your car will will tolerate in the turns.

62 Figure 8

M. Being an Instructor

The instructor gives the student a few final ideas to consider while the student waits for the next run, then hustles over to where today's other student is getting ready for the second try at the course. As she walks, she notices the red Targa with blackout trim pulling onto the course, then charging into the first sweeper. That autocrosser had been a raw rookie just eight months ago, afraid of the car, afraid of the course, wrong tires, and, at first, there hadn't been a cone safe anywhere on the courses. Right now she's waging a spirited campaign to take the lead in her class. "Hmm," she thinks, "you're gonna be a problem and you're in _my_ class."

If you are already an intermediate or expert driver, you will likely be asked to be an instructor at some point. At almost every event there are people eager to learn everything as soon as they can. Someone has to teach them how to do it. This chapter is included to provide you with some food for thought about how best to handle the role of instructor. If you are asked to instruct, and feel that you are a solid and competent driver, reasonably talkative and capable of paying close attention to other people (and not excessively gruff or grumpy), my advice is to jump at the chance. Just because you are not the fastest driver in your club doesn't mean that you can't be a great deal of help to someone who is just starting. If you like to see people learn, instructing can be fun. And, having to explain what you want them to do and why will force you to think more closely about how you drive and which of your own skills might need a little work.

1. Safety: The most important aspect of instructing is to be sure that all instruction happens in a safe environment, and that your students learn to take responsibility for insuring safety at an event. Anytime you see any condition that you think | **Safety is the most important issue** |
unsafe you should stop the proceedings until the condition is fixed. If you should happen to have a student who refuses to drive within reasonable limits, you should take the time for a serious counseling session. If a stern chat fails to correct the situation then you will need to be guided by the policies of your club, but you should not ignore the issue.

Since the risks involved in time trialing are greater, the time trialing instructor will end up spending a great deal of the track time with safety as nearly the only consideration, and will need to assure absolutely that the driving stays within the limits of the student and the car being driven.

2. Car Control: The most important skill being taught is car control. You are responsible for ensuring that your student has sufficient control of the car at ALL times. Obviously, this does not mean that an autocross student won't be doing some slipping, some sliding and some spinning, for certainly these

> *The student __must__ be in control of the car at __all__ times*

will all happen. You should, however, be sure that all of this happens where there is room for it to happen, and that the student has adequate car control and is not frightened. In time trials there is very little room for spinning, and the car needs to be kept within the limits of a very controlled drift.

3. Spacing Your Cars: In autocross, if you are working with more than one student at once, take the initiative to make sure that they are sufficiently separated on the grid. This way each student can have equal access to you, and you will have time to be with each student both before and after each pass at the exercise or each run at the course.

4. Checking the Oil Pressure: Be sure to take occasional glances at the oil light or oil pressure gauge when the car is under hard cornering. Students are often a bit less attentive to the health and maintenance of their car, and they certainly have their hands full of new experiences while they are learning. If there is any sign that the car cannot maintain decent oil pressure under these circumstances you should have the student pull off and begin to determine what steps to take, such as checking the oil level. You are not, of course, responsible for the care of the student's car, but it would be bad to let them trash a motor.

5. Knowing the Tires: Always look at the tires of any student's car before you get in. Be aware of the brand, model and tread condition. Ask the student how much air pressure is in the tires. You won't be surprised Michelin

> *Note the type and condition of the tires*

mud & snow tires won't corner as well as a set of Goodyear Radial T/A R1s, and you should, therefore, keep the speeds of the car consistent with what you expect of the tires that are on the car. You will find out on course what the tires will actually do, but knowing about them in advance will help you gauge how close you are to sliding, and will help you explain to the student why the car won't do everything that the other cars are doing.

6. Paper & Pen: Have a pad of paper and a pen or pencil handy so you can draw while you talk. Drawing clarifies so much of what is going on. Also, once you have scratched all over the paper, be sure to let the student have the paper if he/she wants it. You might be surprised how much your scribbling is valued by a student who wants to sit down later and review the story you are telling.

7. Find Out Why the Student is at the Event: Some people come to an autocross school, or an autocross or a time trial just to learn a little more about driving the car. Some are there because they have been convinced by someone else that it will do them some good. Some think that perhaps they should simply autocross a year before they move up to

> *Some students will get uncomfortable if the car gets at all loose*

Formula 1 racing. Some are experienced competitive drivers trying to get just a little bit better. Some will be interested in everything you can teach them, others will get very uncomfortable if the car gets at all loose. Assessing why they are at the event will help you determine how aggressive they want to be with the car and what they are prepared to learn.

8. Get to Know the Student: First, introduce yourself. As the session progress, tell them a little about yourself. You are about to be very important to these people for a few hours, and they need to feel that they know you.

Second, a little questioning about what they do in real life, their families and especially their hobbies can be very valuable. Both from the way that they talk to you and what they tell you, you can begin to size things up a bit. Hobbies can be especially important. Musicians may hear the tires talking to them before other people. Snow skiers will naturally understand the way in which flat-tracking through a turn will slow them down. Engineers and physicists will understand the details of throttle-on cornering and late apexes.

9. Find Out How Well the Student Knows the Car: In an autocross school or at an autocross, you will occasionally encounter students who have rarely or never driven stick shifts, but who are now driving a borrowed or spouses car with a manual transmission. I have more than once instructed students who were not normally allowed to drive the car by its owner (a spouse or significant other). You should severely decrease the pace of your instruction if the student is having

basic problems operating the machine. This particular problem is not common at time trials.

10. Let the Student Know What is Coming: In the midst of what will be, for many of the students, a true sensory overload, surprises will not be terribly welcome. Let the student know well in advance of new things to do and changes in procedure. Also, let them know what is likely to happen when they do what you tell them to do.

11. Proceed Slowly: Be sure that the student has sufficient mastery of the basic techniques before moving to the fine points. This will help promote a smooth and consistent driving style, critical to the student's success in autocross. In particular, try to move up the speed of each turn in small increments, so the student can detect the onset of handling characteristics such as oversteer and understeer.

12. Be Clear: Sometimes it's easy to forget just how much we have learned from all this competitive driving. Without being condescending, be sure to start at the very beginning and state exactly what you want the student to do. The students will be under a lot of fun-based and self-imposed stress. They will have many new ideas to think about; they may not understand or think about things that seem obvious to you, since their brain is so full of other stuff.

> *Tell them exactly what you want them to do*

13. Have the Students Observe Other Drivers: When track conditions permit it, have your student watch other drivers go through the course or the exercise and explain to you what the other driver is doing well and what is being done less well. To do this your student must observe carefully and formulate these observations into words. You will quickly learn what concepts have been understood well, as well as where you need to place more instructional energy.

14. Self-critique: After the student has a chance to settle down a bit, have him or her tell you what (s)he did right and what was done less right. There are very important reasons for this. First, the student will have to think more intensively about the lesson that is being learned, both to decide what was right and what needed improvement, and to put all this into words to tell you. Second, you can now separate driving

> *Learn to tell the difference between a lack of knowledge and a lack of execution*

problems into those where the student understands what to do but does not yet have the coordination and car control to perform, from areas where the student simply does not understand what is being taught. This separation is important. If the problem is a lack of understanding, then you have to explain better. If the problem is a lack of execution, then either the student just needs more practice, or you need to break down the skill into finer components that the student can master more easily.

Finally, it is critical, from a _motivational_ aspect, that you separate the lack of knowledge from the lack of execution. You need only spend a few moments, at some point in your life, listening to someone explain to you things you know perfectly well, while they fail to answer the questions burning in your mind, to appreciate the nearly-certain fact that you do not ever want to do this to anyone else.

15. BE POSITIVE: This is probably the most important (and difficult) general technique you will need to use. Human beings who are criticized a lot become withdrawn and fearful and tend not to have a very good time. Human beings who are praised a lot become more open, willing to learn and have a very good time.

However, we are putting these human beings into situations where they are going to do almost everything imperfectly, especially at first. What's a poor instructor to do?

The first thing to remember is to try to find EVERYTHING they are doing right, and mention it. Even if they are screwing up the most simple instructions, you could mention to them that it is good that they did not unbuckle their seatbelt and leave the car during the middle of the turn. Find whatever it is that they are doing right, and say something. If they are improving, then you can state things positively no matter how far they still have to go. If they are smooth but slow, tell them they are smooth. If they are erratic but fast, tell them that they are clearly willing to try things (then get to work on staying well within control). If they spin, first tell them what an exciting ride is was, then suggest what they might think about for the next time.

Students are often very self-critical anyway. They may not tell you that they feel like complete klutzes, but they probably do. They are putting themselves into a situation where they are likely to make more 'mistakes' in 30 minutes than they normally make in

> *Most students will be very self-critical;*
> *you need to be positive*

an entire week. It is your job to insure that you do not magnify these feelings of incompetency, but rather tell them all the things they are doing right. Also note:

if you don't tell them the things they are doing right they may well stop doing those things!

Don't underestimate the god-like role you are playing. You know, of course, that you are just you, a regular person trying to help someone learn and enjoy some new skills. For most students, however, the situation looks entirely different. They are in the middle of doing strange and amazing things to their good friend the car. While it does seem fun, this is different from anything they have ever done. And you clearly have been placed in the passenger seat because everyone in the world knows that you know <u>everything</u> about fast driving. Hearing negative statements from you, under these circumstances, will have <u>much</u> <u>more</u> <u>impact</u> than you probably intend.

Good statements include:

> "That was much better than last time."

> "You seem to be learning this very quickly."

> "Have you already done quite a bit of autocrossing?"

> "Your hand position is very nice."

> "That was fun!"

> "You are very smooth."

> "You have excellent control of the car."

> "You recovered from that very nicely."

> "You are clearly willing to charge right into things."

Statements that are not as good include:

> "Don't EVER do that!" (rather, "It's usually best not to slam on the brakes in the middle of a turn.")

> "That was a bad run." (rather, "Well, you've done better. It's very normal to be a little uneven at first. And, you did a great job of . . . The important things to think about before the next run are . . .")

If you can get to where you have made 4 or 5 positive statements for every neutral or negative statement that you have to make, and if you can couch the corrective statements in gentle terms ("Let's see if we can . . . ", or "Things could work out a little bit better if . . .") you will find that your students learn much faster and have a much better time.

16. Talk to the Student: Don't get into the habit of just riding in the car and observing. Yes, the student is quite busy right now. Yes, the student can't possibly pay careful attention to everything you want to say, right now, as the student is very busy. Just tell the students before you head out onto the course or the exercise that you will be talking a lot, and that they should hang on to whatever ideas they can, and let the rest float right on by. And that, if there should be something that they <u>really</u> need to act on right away, you'll be sure to get their attention. Tell them that you will also discuss the entire run once the run is finished.

First, it's a bit intimidating for the students to have you sitting there like a rock. Seems like they must be doing terribly. Second, they really can hear some of what you say, even while they are really concentrating on the driving. What they <u>do</u> pick up from you, they can put to immediate use. It also makes it easier for you to reconstruct events later if you can use phrases like, "Do you remember when I yelled, 'BRAKES!!?' Well, the key thing about that turn was . . ." As the students get used to concentrating on driving and listening with one ear, you will be able to guide them with confidence into some of the more difficult skills.

17. Have a Good Time Yourself: Instructing can be a great deal of fun if you let it. The students are usually very keen to learn. You will find yourself in some cars that really aren't ready to perform very well, but that doesn't mean the student can't learn the basic techniques. After a full day or weekend of jumping

> *Instructing can be incredibly rewarding, if you let it*

in and out of cars, tracking down students, doing your own driving and perhaps helping to set up and tear down the track, you might be quite weary. However, there is a special thrill, for me, at least, of watching the fun the students have, as they begin to grasp the concepts and apply them, as a difficult corner becomes understood and can be taken on a clean line at the limits of the car's ability. The joy continues when you run into these people at other events in your area, and see how much their skills have developed, remembering that you are at least partly responsible for getting them off to a good start.

N. Final Thoughts

Once you get completely hooked on this sport, remember to stay close to the small-club events. It is easy, if you are dedicated and a little talented, to get yourself involved in several season-long racing series'. Championship points, counted toward year-end trophies, become important, and schedules begin to revolve around points events. Remember why you got into all this in the first place. Make time to go to 'fun' events that are not well attended. There won't be 150 people to see you make that great run, but you can drive just for the sheer pleasure of experiencing the car doing what it likes to do. You will get more runs, pick up valuable practice time, and stay in touch with the fundamentals of the sport.

If you become an avid competitor, you may begin to notice that the sport has very definite rhythms. There are circles within circles and patterns within patterns, a process that is nearly biologic in richness and interconnectedness.

At the finest detail, each turn has its rhythm; braking before the entry, then getting the car into the turn and settled; passing the apex and feeding the power; finally, drifting out to the exit and beginning to concentrate on the next turn. The turns link up to create the rhythm of the lap. You find yourself in a nearly hypnotic rhythm, moving from one turn to the next, dancing to the beat of the course as it lies. Turn 1 . . . then turn 2 . . . a little straight then turn 3 . . . Finally, the turns add up to a lap. The laps (if you run more than one) are the beat of the run. First lap practice, settle in and find what the car and the course want. Second lap, execute sharply, keeping the pressure on. Final lap, stay gutsy and precise, but don't blow a good run by reaching for something that isn't there.

The days have their own rhythm, from the early alarm clock and sleepy drive, to the moving-in process of getting settled and ready to compete. Lunch as it happens, temperature warming during the day. Finally the end of the day, when many duels have been settled, but the most interesting are still on the line. In these classes any run can establish a new leader, or move the current leader further from those who would challenge. The rhythmic beats of the day are the runs you make. Interspersed with the constant flow of cars onto and off the course, you ease into the line of ready cars, make your run, get your time and ease back to your waiting place, a flow that comes to seem as natural as a river.

The years have their own racing rhythm as well. Slow in the winter, preparing and beginning in the spring, hot days in the summer, final events, maybe with the year's championship hanging in the balance, during the fall. Then it all cycles again. You find yourself feeling the rhythms like a subtle, quiet music, and they guide you through the year.

There are much worse things than finding yourself living to the tune of this music. There may be times when you wonder whether it's worth the effort, the long days, the expensive tires the careful attention to every detail. There are more times, though, when you wonder if there will ever be anything else you enjoy so much, and what you would have done with your life if you hadn't stumbled into this.

Don't get too discouraged in the beginning. There's a lot to learn. If you want it, you will have it. It just takes time and dedication. Don't overestimate the differences between machines. Yes, good car preparation is essential, but, until you have some real expertise, more time will be gained by learning to drive than by modifying the car. On the other hand, once you think you are getting pretty good at this, don't expect to beat competent drivers who are riding in superior machinery. If you want to win a truly competitive class, you have to have your car in top shape; remember, if you want to move a mountain it's always a good idea to bring a steam shovel along.

Stay safe, and may all your apexes be precise.

Appendix 1, Glossary

Apex: n., the point at which you come the closest to the inside of the turn. Same as <u>clipping point</u>.

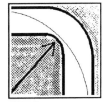

Autocross: n., the sport of driving cars a fixed number of laps on a pylon-defined course with the goal of completing the run in a minimum of time without moving any pylons.

63 *Apex*

Banked: adj., refers to turns which are sloped so as to help the car stay on the track, high on the outside.

Bench Racing: n., the process of discussing the race afterwards or before, usually sitting on a bench at a pizza parlor.

Berm: n., a raised portion at the edge of a turn, often of concrete. You may run over part of it if your car doesn't object.

Black Flag: n., used at time trials to bring a specific driver off the course for a chat with the officials. If furled, it is a warning; the driver does not have to exit the course. If displayed with the driver's number, the driver must come in.

CMC: proper noun, Council of Motorsports Clubs. Devoted to staging national-level autocross events.

Camber: n., the extent to which a tire is not perpendicular to the ground. Measured in degrees. Negative camber is the top of the tire being closer to the center of the car than the bottom of the tire. Positive camber is the reverse.

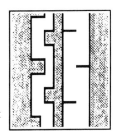

Caster: n., the extent to which the turning axis of the tire is not vertical. The pivot of a front tire is an axis that points at the ground <u>ahead</u> of where the tire touches the ground.

64 *Two Chicanes*

Checkered Flag: n., used to show the run is over; the driver must exit the course.

Chicane: (shi•KANE) n., a series of S-shaped bends in the course. Also called Esses.

Chunk: v.i. the process of a tire loosing small portions (chunks) of rubber from the tread area.

Class: n., a group of cars that were relatively similar when manufactured and have been modified to about the same degree. Organizing competition by classes allows entrants to run against cars of similar capability.

Clipping Point: n., the point where the car touches the inside of the turn. Apex.

Cone: n., pylon. Orange traffic marker used to define an autocross course.

Corner: a) n. turn. b) v.i. the process of turning a car, as in cornering. c) n. a portion of the car, as in "the left front corner isn't sticking."

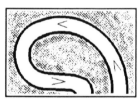

Corrected Time: n., total time plus pylon penalties.

Courseworker: n., a person on the course setting up pylons and assuring safety.

Cross-over: n., a point at which the course crosses over itself.

65 *Cross-over*

Decreasing-radius Turn: n., a turn that begins gently and becomes more severe (sharper).

Deep: v.i., going very far into a turn before braking; e.g. "He out-deeped me in that turn."

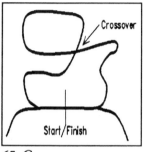

Dirt-track: v.i., cornering with a large amount of oversteer (tail of the car hanging out to the outside of a corner), as in, "I dirt-tracked my way around the entire sweeper." Often not the

66 *Decreasing-Radius Turn*

fastest way around through a turn, as the car may be exceeding the optimum slip angle of the rear tires. Synonymous with flat-track, used as a verb.

DNF (Did Not Finish): n., a run that was not properly completed, or during which the driver violated certain rules that invalidate the run (such as having all four wheels of the car off course and failing to re-enter the course where the car originally went off course).

Double Clutch: v.i. the process of shifting (usually shifting down one or more gears) which uses the following sequence: depress clutch, shift transmission into neutral, release clutch, (depress throttle briefly if downshifting, to get engine speed to match the engine speed that will be required once the clutch is ultimately released in the new gear), depress clutch, move transmission into the new gear, release clutch.

Downshift: v.t. shifting the transmission to a lower gear.

Drift: v.t. the process of cornering a car under control, but at the very limits of adhesion, with the tires moving slightly sideways. The sensation is one of 'drifting' slightly to the side while charging through the turn.

Early: v.t. cornering with an early-apex line, as in "I earlied turn 3."

Early Apex: n., any apex that occurs (or could occur) before the geometric apex. Also, v.t. ("He early-apexed that turn.")

Entrance (to a turn): n., the point at which you start turning the steering wheel into the turn. Normally the entrance is on the opposite side from the direction you will turn (start from the far right before entering a left-hand turn). Same as turn-in-point.

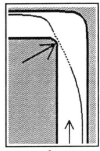

67 Early Apex

Ergonomics: n., the science of the interaction of physical beings with their physical surroundings.

Esses: n., a series of S-shaped bends in the course. Also called a chicane.

Exit (from a turn): n., the point at which you have completed a turn (normally opposite from the direction of the turn - after a left-hand turn you will normally end up on the right side of the course) and are beginning to set up for the next turn.

Exit Lane: n., the lane provided for the driver to exit the course.

Field Trials: n., an autocross with hilly terrain, often on an unpaved surface.

Flagperson: n., person who stands at the start/finish line and directs traffic onto and off the course.

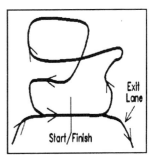

68 Exit Lane

Flatspot: n., a section of the tread of a tire that has been prematurely worn down due to excessive use of brakes or dramatic slides. Refers to the tire being flat rather than round at this particular spot. Does not refer to a loss of air pressure in the tire. Also, v.t., as in "I really flatspotted the front tires."

<u>Flat-track</u>: v.i., cornering with a large amount of oversteer (tail of the car hanging out to the outside of a corner), as in, "I flat-tracked my way around that hairpin." Not usually the fastest way around through a turn, as the car is probably exceeding the optimum slip angle of the rear tires. Synonymous with <u>dirt-track</u>, used as a verb.

<u>Friction Circle</u>: n., diagram that shows the extent to which a tire may brake and turn at the same time. A tire may operate <u>anywhere</u> on or within the circle.

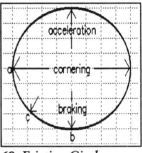

69 Friction Circle

<u>Fun Autocross</u>: n., autocross not counting toward year-end points. Of course, all autocrosses are fun as long as the weather isn't completely rotten and the competitors are not tense with each other. This is to distinguish such autocrosses from <u>points autocrosses</u>. By way of example, a club may start the year with one or two fun autocrosses, then stage a series of seven or so points autocrosses. Only the results of the points autocrosses will count toward the year-end trophies.

<u>Fun-run</u>: n., a run that does not officially count as a competitive run for the day. Entrants who do not sign up to run in a specific class are usually considered to be making fun-runs each time they run. Additionally, under certain formats (four run groups, for example) it is not uncommon for everyone in the run group to have made their allotted two or three runs and still have some of the time allotted to this run group left over. In such cases people often are offered fun-runs which will not count toward the competition of the day. Often a small charge ($1) will be levied for each fun-run.

<u>Gate</u>: n., a pair (or more) of pylons through which you must drive and which define the course. Used extensively when the course edges are not lined. Also, n., starting gate. The beginning portion of the course where one or two cars wait to be flagged onto the course.

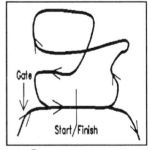

70 Gate

<u>Geometric Apex</u>: n., the point at which an arc of constant radius (the largest one that will fit) will touch the inside of the turn.

<u>Green Flag</u>: n., go. Signal the driver onto the course and shows, when the driver passes start/finish, that the driver should continue driving the course.

<u>Grid</u>: n., the staging area where cars wait for their runs. Also called <u>pregrid</u>.

Hillclimb: n., the sport of driving an uphill road for time, with cars spaced out to prevent passing situations. Normally on a public road which is closed to normal traffic for this event. This is effectively a time trial up a hill.

Heel and Toe: v.i., method of downshifting in which the left foot depresses the clutch and the right foot operates both the brake and the throttle.

Hot Lap(s): n., timed laps not preceded by a practice lap.

Increasing-radius Turn: n., a turn that begins tight and becomes more gentle (less severe).

Late Apex: n., any apex that occurs (or could occur) after the geometric apex. Also, v.t., ("He late-apexed that turn very nicely.")

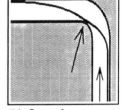

71 Late Apex

Lift: v.i., to remove one's foot from the throttle.

Line: n., the path taken through a turn or several turns.

Marbles: n., gravel on the course, usually where most drivers are not choosing to drive.

Off-camber: adj., refers to turns where the road is sloped toward the outside of the turn, making it more difficult for the car to stick to the road surface.

Official Re-run: n., an additional run given to a competitor when the first run did not work out due to conditions not under the control of the driver. Such conditions include the failure of timing equipment (mechanical, electronic or human) during a run, or having been red-flagged because some other car on course had some manner of difficulty. Sometimes simply called a re-run.

Overlap: n., the condition in which two cars are on the course at the same time. This normally occurs as a car is about halfway through its last timed lap and the next car is flagged onto the course to begin its practice lap. However, with enough timing equipment and good timers it is possible to run overlap when cars are being allowed only one hot lap.

Oversteer: n., the condition under which a car is turning more rapidly than would be caused by the extent to which the steering wheel has been turned. It is due to the rear wheels loosing traction and sliding toward the outside of the turn which points the nose of the car increasingly toward the center of the turn more than the driver is turning the steering wheel.

Plow: n., v.i. See 'understeer'.

Points Autocross: n., an autocross the results of which count toward series points. This is to distinguish such autocrosses from fun autocrosses. By way of example, a club may start the year with one or two fun autocrosses, then stage a series of seven or so points autocrosses. Only the results of the points autocrosses will count toward the year-end trophies.

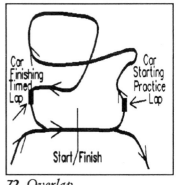

Posting: v.t., the activity of writing official times on sheets posted for all to read.

72 Overlap

Power Point: n., the point at which you begin depressing the throttle to accelerate out of the turn.

Practice Lap: n., a lap on the course during which the clock is not running and pylons you hit do not count.

Practice Session: n., a period of time during which a run group of time trial cars practice together on the track.

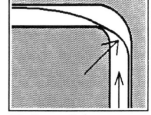

73 Power Point

Pre-grid: n., the staging area where cars wait for their runs. Also called grid.

Pro-Solo: proper n., a national series of autocrosses (about 12 per year) sponsored by SCCA. The Pro-Solo events feature comparatively high entry fees, cash prizes, and a course designed as start-here-finish-there, with two mirror-image sides, so two competitors can run head-to-head at the same time.

Push: n., understeer. The tendency of the nose of the car to continue traveling in a straight line despite the steering wheel being turned.

Pylon Count: n., the number of pylons knocked over or knocked completely out of the box drawn on the road surface to mark their proper location.

Pylon Penalty: n., the total amount of time added to a score. This is usually one second for each pylon knocked over or out of its box.

Pyrometer: n., device for measuring temperature; especially tire temperature. Used to determine precise tire pressure and suspension alignments.

Red Flag: **EVERYONE STOP NOW!!!**. n., used to tell drivers to stop the car IMMEDIATELY and await further instructions from course workers or the flagperson. Used when an unsafe condition exists. Also, v.t., to use a red flag.

Red-line: n., the engine speed (in revolutions per minute, RPM) which should not be exceeded lest serious engine damage result. Usually marked on the tachometer. Many cars have a rev-limiter to prevent exceeding red-line.

Registration: n., the place where entrants register for the event. Involves filling out forms and paying money. Also the process of registering.

Re-run: n., an additional run given to a competitor when the first run did not work out due to conditions not under the control of the driver. Such conditions include the failure of timing equipment (mechanical, electronic or human), or having been red-flagged. Sometimes also called an official re-run.

Rev-limiter: n., a device that mechanically or electrically limits engine speed to a certain RPM.

Run Group: n., a grouping of cars that will be making their runs during the same block of time, or, in time trials, that will be practicing together.

SCCA: proper n., Sports Car Club of America. Large club devoted to providing opportunities for various forms of automotive, non-dragstrip performance competition.

Scratch Time: n., the time spent on timed laps (without any pylon penalties being added).

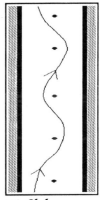

74 *Slalom*

Second Driver: n., a second (or third or fourth) person driving the same car.

Second Driver Car: n., any car being used by more than one driver.

Second Driver Line: n., the line on the grid used by second drivers.

Short-shift: v.t., Shifting the transmission into a higher gear before the normal shift point.

Slalom: n., a portion of the course where the car must weave back and forth between pylons that have been set up in the middle of the course. Also, n., another name for autocross.

Slip Angle: n., the difference, in degrees, between the direction a tire is pointed and the direction it is traveling. May also be applied to an entire vehicle.

Solo I: proper n., <u>SCCA</u> term for <u>time trials</u>.

Solo II: proper n., <u>SCCA</u> term for <u>autocross</u>.

<u>Spin</u>: n., the process of the car spinning around 180° or more.

<u>Split-time</u>: n., the elapsed time of the first lap, when two timed laps are being run. Also called 'split'.

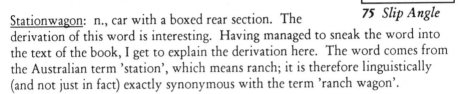

75 Slip Angle

<u>Stationwagon</u>: n., car with a boxed rear section. The derivation of this word is interesting. Having managed to sneak the word into the text of the book, I get to explain the derivation here. The word comes from the Australian term 'station', which means ranch; it is therefore linguistically (and not just in fact) exactly synonymous with the term 'ranch wagon'.

<u>Start/finish</u>: n., the point on the course where the car will start the clocks when beginning the run and stop the clock at the end of the run.

<u>Starting Gate</u>: n., the beginning portion of the course where one or two cars wait to be flagged onto the course. Also called <u>gate</u>.

<u>Sweeper</u>: n., a relatively gentle, higher-speed turn of more than 90°.

<u>Tech</u>: v.t., the process of safety-inspecting a car. Also, n., the place where such inspection is done. Shortened form of <u>technical</u> <u>inspection</u>.

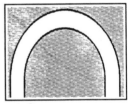

76 Sweeper

<u>Technical Inspection</u>: n., a safety inspection of a car.

<u>Time Trials</u>: n., an event held on a roadracing course where cars run individually for time but do not race wheel-to-wheel.

<u>Timed Lap</u>: n., a lap around the course during which a car is timed. When two or more laps are run it is most common to have the score be calculated as the sum of the two laps in autocross, but to count each lap individually in time trials.

<u>Timing</u>: v.t., the process of measuring the time each car takes for its timed laps. Also, n., the place where timing is done.

<u>Timing Slip</u>: n., a small piece of paper usually given to each driver after a run showing the <u>split-time</u>, <u>scratch time</u>, <u>pylon penalty</u> and <u>total time</u>.

<u>Torque</u>: v. to set or check the tightness of a nut, especially a wheel lug nut.

Total Time: n., the total of time spent on timed laps plus the penalties for any pylons knocked over or moved out of their box. Same as <u>corrected time</u>.

Trail-braking: v.i., continuing to apply some brakes while beginning a turn.

Turn: n., a bend in the course. See illustration.

Turn-in-Point: n., point at which the car begins a turn. Same as entrance (to a turn).

Upshift: v.t., shifting the transmission to a higher gear.

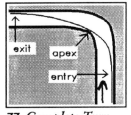

77 Complete Turn

Understeer: n., The condition under which the car is continuing to travel relatively straight ahead despite the front wheels being turned, due to lack of sufficient traction at the front tires. Also called 'plowing' or 'pushing'.

Wheel-to-Wheel: adj., describes any form of racing where the entrants are on the track at the same time and are trying to pass each other during the contest. Does not apply to autocross or time trials.

Appendix 2, Bibliography

There is a natural overlap of information among autocrossing, time trials and roadracing, since much of the theory of car preparation and car control is the same. This is fortunate, since there are many books about roadracing and almost none about solo racing. The useful content of these books varies greatly. Many are written by famous and successful racers, sometimes with the help of a professional writer. There are usually lots of photos of the general type "Here I am passing Nikki Lauda (or Bob Bondurant or Barney Olfield) at Le Mans (or Monaco or the Grass Valley 1/4-mile Dirt Oval.") This is great if you are a fan of the author, but doesn't necessarily help you learn competitive driving. Each book has, however, something to recommend it, be it just a page or two on suspension theory, proper lines, ergonomics or whatever. Of course, the sections on passing other drivers, handling pit crews, etc., while interesting enough, are not relevant to autocrossing or time trials.

The best sources of publications dealing with cars and driving are the mailorder houses that specialize in automotive books. Classic Motorbooks (800-826-6600) is the largest of these and their catalog contains a wealth of information. Classic is also the publisher of many important automotive books. Other mailorder businesses, such as Discount Book Company, 415-454-3122, Toad Hall Motorbooks, 303-235-0116, John Dragich Discount Auto Literature, 800-328-8484, Automobile Quarterly, 215-375-8444, Auto Book Center, 508-832-6438, and 401-351-5970 and Albion Scott Motorbooks, 212-980-1928, also specialize in automotive books, and you may wish to check to see what they have available.

If your interest is in motor-tuning information, there are plenty of books on the topic generally and on specific motors.

There are separate sections below for books and videos. Items are presented in approximately the order in which I would recommend them, but people's tastes in such matters vary a great deal, so you may want to check out several of the books and videos listed. All books are paperback unless otherwise noted.

BOOKS

<u>Bob Bondurant on High Performance Driving</u>; Bob Bondurant with John Blakemore; 1987, Motorbooks International, 144 pages, $12.95. One of the better books you will find. Offers an excellent section on ergonomics and lots of good information on many topics. Very balanced and very complete.

<u>The Art of Motor Racing</u>; Emerson Fittipaldi & Gordon Kirby; 1987, Nutmeg Productions, 144 pages, $19.95. A delightful book for Emo affectionados, with plenty of life-philosophy, and includes a great deal of good counsel about driving techniques. Also has a good glossary and an excellent bibliography.

<u>Driving in Competition</u>; Alan Johnson; 1971, Norton Press, 156 pages, $8.95. This is an excellent book. Mostly about roadracing, it includes a very nice treatment of selecting the right line through a series of corners.

<u>The Technique of Motor Racing</u>, Piero Taruffi; 1958, Robert Bently Press, Cambridge, Mass, $25.00. This classic book was out of print for a long time, but has just been republished by Bently Press. Taruffi was a Formula 1 engineer for Ferrari who set out to explain everything. Call 800-423-4595 to order.

<u>How to Make your Car Handle</u>; Fred Puhn; 1981, HP Books, 200 pages, $12.95. An absolutely indispensable work on automotive suspension systems. More than most people will want to know, but has everything. Written in a very straight-forward style, with occasional and delightful dry humor. It is not at the top of my list only because not everyone wants to read about suspensions.

<u>Expert Driving</u>; Patrick Bedard; 1987, Valentine Research, 80 pages, $9.95. A relatively short book that discusses basic driving skills and the use of the <u>g-analyst</u>. The publisher is the company that manufacturers and markets the <u>g-analyst</u>. It is a book about smoothness in controlling a car, written with a lyrical and passionate style by a driving expert who cares about the topic. Well worth reading.

<u>Driving to Win</u>; Al Holbert & Bob Holbert; 1982, Aztex Corporation, 128 pages, $7.95. Includes a good analysis of maximizing performance in any given turn, otherwise is mostly about SCCA road-racing.

The Art and Science of Grand Prix Driving; Niki Lauda; 1975, Motorbooks International, 245 pages, $21.95, hardbound. The best of this book, for our purposes, is the information on suspension. Also points out certain aspects of slip angle.

Jackie Stewart's Principles of Performance Driving; Jackie Stewart & Alan Henry; 1986, Hazleton Publishing, 248 pages, $29.95, hardbound. There are not exactly a large number of principles in here, but there is some interesting information on suspension. It is pleasant reading.

Brake Handbook; Fred Puhn, 1985, HP Books, 176 Pages, $12.95. More than most solo racers will need to know about brakes, but a careful and thorough tome that can be used as a reference. Time trialers will sooner or later end up needing to know what the brakes are up to, and this is the help they will need.

Winning Autocross Solo II Competition; Richard Turner & J. B. Miles; 1977, Turner Design, 128 pages, $8.95. There are important differences between Turner's book and the one you are currently holding, both in opinion and fact. Also, the tone of the book is a bit too heavy handed and rah-rah for my tastes. However, if you are serious about the sport of autocross, there are some good tips here and it is worth the money and time.

Superdriver: Exercises for High-Concentration, High-Performance Driving - A Tune-Up Kit for the Mind; Sir John Whitmore; 1988, Motorbooks International, 64 pages, $9.95. This is not about cornering techniques. It is about mental preparation and the mental side of driving. I couldn't get into it, but if you can it will probably help you.

VIDEO GAMES

Hard Drivin', by Atari. $.50 for 1.6 minutes. This is an amazing driving simulator disguised as a video game. It offers impressive visual, tactile and audible realism. You won't learn much about lines, as most of the non-stunt turns are long sweepers and you don't have much choice about where to drive. You will get a real feel for the delicate adjustment of slip angle at high speeds. The machine will also bite you severely if you are not very smooth with the controls, making it a good time trial simulator. The best approach: sit down with $10 worth of quarters and see if you can get your score into the 50,000 range. There aren't many places you can get track time for $20/hour, so don't worry about the quarters. A word of caution: take a break before you drive home. If you get very involved in the game, you may find yourself driving the same way on the street.

VIDEOS

You may be able to rent the videos for a lot less than it costs to buy them. You're not likely to find them in the video rental shops in your local mall, but the better race-supply shops will often have them. If you don't know where such a shop is near you, check the yellow pages under Automobile Performance Racing & Sports Car Equipment.

Going Faster (Skip Barber); 90-minute video, $79.95. This is an incredibly good video, the best of the bunch. It is oriented around drivers learning to roadrace open wheel cars at Barber's school at Lime Rock, but the first 40 minutes is devoted to competitive driving material that is equally relevant to solo racing. Skip and his instructors start at the beginning and tell you almost everything you need to know about how to drive safely at speed. Special sections include racing in the rain, front-wheel drive cars and the normal way flags are used on the roadrace tracks. Don't miss this one.

Behind the Wheel with Jackie Stewart; 60-minute video, $59.95. This video is oriented toward street driving, but has some very nice content for the aspiring competitive driver. Includes some very interesting footage of vintage car races at Laguna Seca. Some of the presentation order is muddy, but Stewart ultimately gets his message across. In this video he comes across as a much more personable chap than in his book, and he even includes clips of his own accidents (one of them twice!). This is a pleasant and educational sixty minutes. If you get this one, watch his approach to hand control.

Drive to Win with Mario Andretti; 2-hour video, 1988, $49.95. In addition to being devoted to instruction, this video also serves as a bit of a personality profile of Andretti. The instruction content is based on the Russell driving school. It has a good explanation of the balance of friction, using the friction circle as a basis, and has a nice discussion of balancing tire slip and drag for maximum speeds through corners. It also covers how going uphill or downhill changes your approach to line selection and driving techniques. There is much overlap between this and the Skip Barber video, but you may want to watch both if you are trying to soak up everything. This one, while good, isn't as tightly organized or efficient with your time.

<u>Autocrossing with Dick Turner</u>; 1-hour video, $49.95. This is the only video available on autocrossing, and it's a real shame it isn't better. While it is correct in some instances, and it will give the beginner a look at a certain style of autocrossing, it is wrong often enough to confuse some very basic issues. If you are an avid autocrosser, you may want to take a look. Just remember that, when things aren't making sense, it may not be due to any inability on your part. Rather, it is probably because the stuff being presented <u>doesn't</u> make sense.

<u>Sports Car Experience</u>; Powersports Video (818-907-0590), 1987; 60-minute video. This video consists of footage shot from the driver's perspective in the cockpit. The cockpit in question is mostly a Porsche 956 racecar. The tracks covered are Silverstone, Hochheim, Spa, Fuji, Kuala Lumpur and Le Mans. Included are one crash and a spin at Le Mans. There is little narration and the music is inane. This won't teach you much about driving; it will just show you a driver's view of these events.

<u>Power Basics of Auto Racing Video Tape</u>; Parnelli Jones; 78-minute video, 1984; $49.95. This video was a real disappointment. It is ill-organized, and much of the content is not relevant to effective driving. Some of the demonstrations are presented in ways that are potentially misleading. Also features a driver in a racing suit but no helmet, showing techniques that are supposed to be at speed and that are being done on a race track; this is a very bad example to set. Save your money.

CAR CLUBS & MAGAZINES & OTHER STUFF

<u>MARQUE CLUBS</u>: If your car was built with high-speed performance and handling in mind, it is a good bet that there is a national club for it, and that the club organizes autocrosses, slaloms and perhaps time trials. This obviously includes cars such as Corvettes, Ferraris, Porsches, the Z-series Nissans, Fieros and many others, but also extends to companies such as BMW, Honda, and Saab. You will also find the people in the club who are interested in racing to be invaluable sources of information about what your car wants to have done to it so it can be a happy camper while motoring around a course. You will normally get some sort of monthly newsletter or magazine. In some cases you will get a newsletter from your local group, and a glossy magazine sent to all members nationwide. To find your club, check with the car dealer, or look in the back of a magazine such as <u>Road & Track</u> or <u>Car & Driver</u>.

<u>SCCA</u>: SCCA sponsors road-races, autocrosses (Solo-II) and time trials (Solo-I) at both regional and national levels across the United States. It is a very large organization, about 52,000 members, dedicated to competitive motorsports. You

will be welcome driving just about brand of car in any state of modification, as long as it is safe. Because SCCA must cope with such a diversity of cars, you will find yourself running against a variety of brands of automobiles. They do their best, within the inevitable politics that accompanies running such a diverse organization, to group cars fairly. Many events are very well attended, so you may get somewhat less time on the track than with small events run by a marque club. You will get a national magazine as well as a regional newsletter to keep you up to date on all the events coming up and the results of recent events. You can call 303-694-7222 for further information, or write to SCCA, P.O. Box 3278, Englewood, Colorado 80155.

CMC: Rather newly organized (1988), the Council of Motorsports Clubs is composed of 40 different car clubs, most of them marque-oriented clubs. Its primary function is to organize a national-level series of events (12 or so is the current goal) similar to SCCA Pro-Solo. Car classification follows SCCA rather closely, making it easy for SCCA competitors to fit well into a class. CMC is not involved in organize local-club autocrosses, since the member clubs can do this for themselves. Grassroots Motorsports magazine owns this sanctioning body. You may contact CMC at P.O. Drawer C, Daytona Beach, Florida 32118, or 904-676-2424.

Special Purpose Clubs: There is a hillclimb association that sponsors what are effectively time trials consisting of a run from the bottom of a mountain to the top. There are also vintage racing societies that stage races in which you are expected to be especially careful not to bump anyone's irreplaceable fenders. It shouldn't take much sleuthing to find out which such clubs are active in your area.

There are many sport-oriented automotive magazines. The best of these, such as Road & Track, AutoWeek, Car & Driver and Automobile will have plenty of valuable information for the solo racer.

One magazine has solo racing as its primary focus. It is called Grassroots Motorsports (formerly Auto-X and Grassroots Motorsports). The mailing address is drawer A, Daytona Beach, Florida 32118. The street address is 425 Parque Drive, Ormond Beach, Florida 32174. Their phone is 904-673-4148. It sets as its domain Solo-I, Solo-II, Pro-Solo, vintage racing, hill climbs, rallying and ice racing. Subscriptions, as of this writing, are $14.97/year.

Potshots: The Pot-Shots used in the time trial chapter are but two of the hundreds available. They are postcards with a drawing and a small epigram. Ashleigh Brilliant has been described as the worlds only full-time professional epigramist, and he has written some very interesting stuff. For a sample set of postcards and a complete catalog, send $2 to Brilliant Enterprises, 117 West Valerio Street, Santa Barbara, California 93101.

Index

Henry Watts is an electronics manufacturing consultant, living in Sunnyvale, California. He has been autocrossing and time trialing in California for several years. He is a time trial instructor, holds two class lap records at Laguna Seca Raceway and has won many class championships. In 1989 he was the Chairman of the Autocross School for the Porsche Club of America, Zone 7. This is his second book.